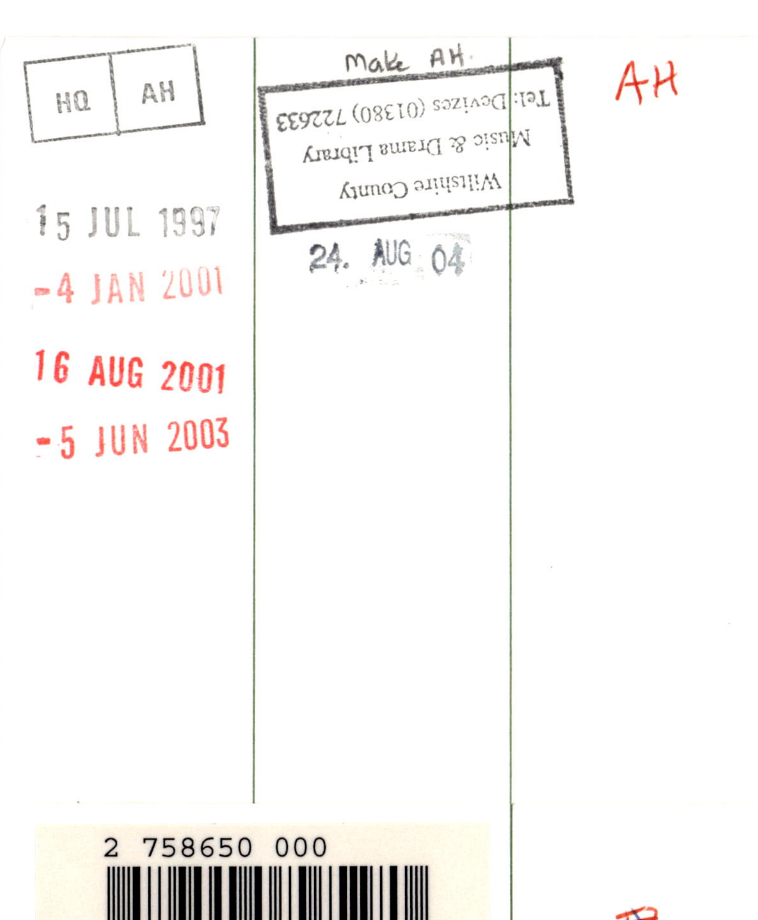
HQ
AH
Make AH.
AH
Wiltshire County
Music & Drama Library
Tel: Devizes (01380) 722633
15 JUL 1997
-4 JAN 2001
16 AUG 2001
-5 JUN 2003
24. AUG 04

2 758650 000

Exclusive distributors:
Music Sales Australia Pty. Limited
120 Rothschild Avenue, Rosebery, NSW 2018.

ISBN 0.949785.13.X
Order No. MS1928

Art direction by Mike Bell (UK).
Cover illustration by Gordon Thompson (UK).
Artwork by Terry Middlin
Illustrations by Frank Gapinski
Typeset by Capital Setters (UK).
Printed in Australia by Robert Burton Printers Pty. Limited.

Music Sales complete catalogue lists thousands of titles and is free from your local music book shop, or direct from Music Sales Pty. Limited, PO Box Q78, Queen Victoria Building, Sydney, NSW2000.

Arrangements by Mike Jackson

1
All I Want For Cwithmath

Words & Music by Don Gardner

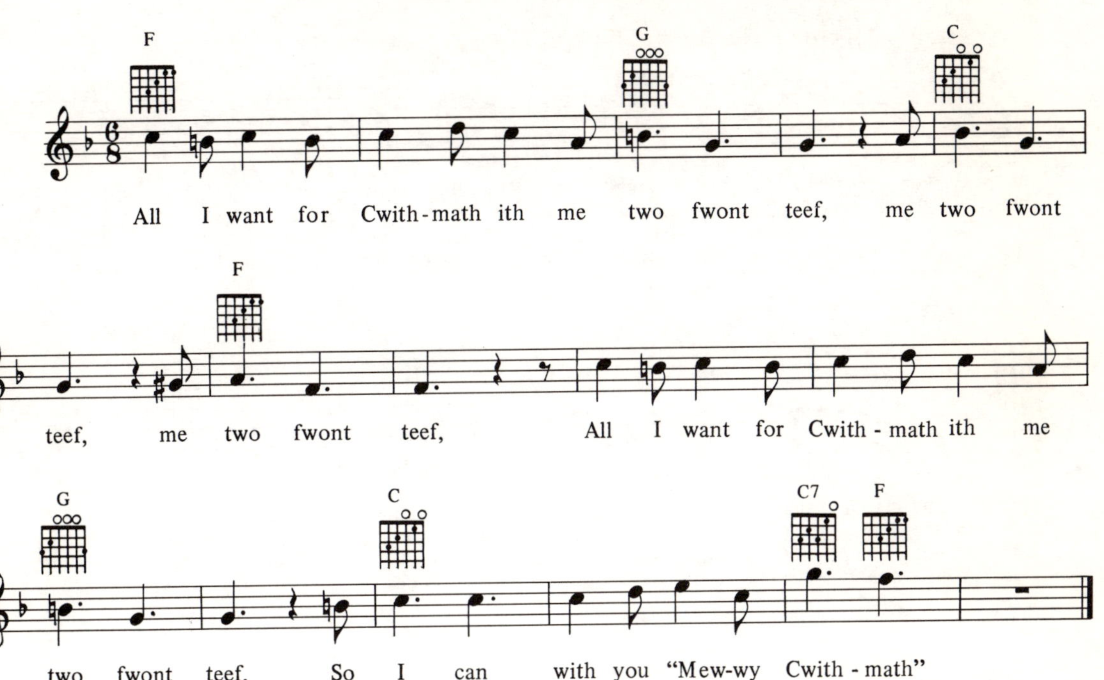
F G C
All I want for Cwith-math ith me two fwont teef, me two fwont
F
teef, me two fwont teef, All I want for Cwith - math ith me
G C C7 F
two fwont teef, So I can with you "Mew-wy Cwith - math"

2

The Ants Came Marching

Traditional/Arranged by Mike Jackson

Am C
1. The ants came mar - ching one by one, Hurr - ah! Hurr - ah! The
2. The ants came mar - ching two by two, Hurr - ah! Hurr - ah! The
3. The ants came mar - ching three by three, Hurr - ah! Hurr - ah! The
4. The ants came mar - ching four by four, Hurr - ah! Hurr - ah! The
Am C E
ants came march - ing one by one, Hurr - ah! Hurr - ah! The
ants came march - ing two by two, Hurr - ah! Hurr - ah! The
ants came march - ing three by three, Hurr - ah! Hurr - ah! The
ants came march - ing four by four, Hurr - ah! Hurr - ah! The
C G Am E7
ants came marching one by one - The little one stopped to suck his thumb. They
ants came marching two by two - The little one stopped to tie his shoe. They
ants came marching three by three - The little one stopped to climb a tree. They
ants came marching four by four - The little one stopped to shut the door. They
Am G F E Am E
all go march - ing down a -round the town. (Boom. boom, boom.)
all go march - ing down a -round the town. (Boom, boom, boom.)
all go march - ing down a- round the town. (Boom, boom, boom.)
all go march - ing down a -round the town. (Boom, boom, boom.)

The ants came marching five by five. . .
The little one stopped to take a dive. . .

The ants came marching six by six. . .
The little one stopped to pick up sticks. . .

The ants came marching seven by seven. . .
The little one stopped to go to heaven. . .

The ants came marching eight by eight. . .
The little one stopped to shut the gate. . .

The ants came marching nine by nine. . .
The little one stopped to scratch his spine.

The ants came marching ten by ten. . .
The little one stopped to say THE END.

3

Away In A Manger

Anon/Arranged by Mike Jackson

G D G E7 Am D7

1. A-way in a — man-ger, no — crib for a bed, The — lit-tle Lord
2. The cat-tle are — low-ing, the — ba-by a wakes. But — lit-tle Lord
3. Be near me, Lord — Jes-us; I — ask thee to stay Close — by me for

G A7 D G D G

Jes-us lay — down his sweet head. The stars in the — bright sky looked —
Jes-us no — cry-ing he makes. I love thee, Lord — Jes-us! Look —
ev-er, and — love me, I pray. Bless all the dear — child-ren in —

E7 Am D7 G Am D G

down where he lay, The — lit-tle Lord Jes-us a-sleep on the hay.
down from the sky. And — stay by my bed-side till — morn-ing is nigh.
thy ten-der care And — fit us for heav-en to — live with thee there.

4
Baa Baa Black Sheep

Traditional/Additional Words: Mike & Michelle Jackson

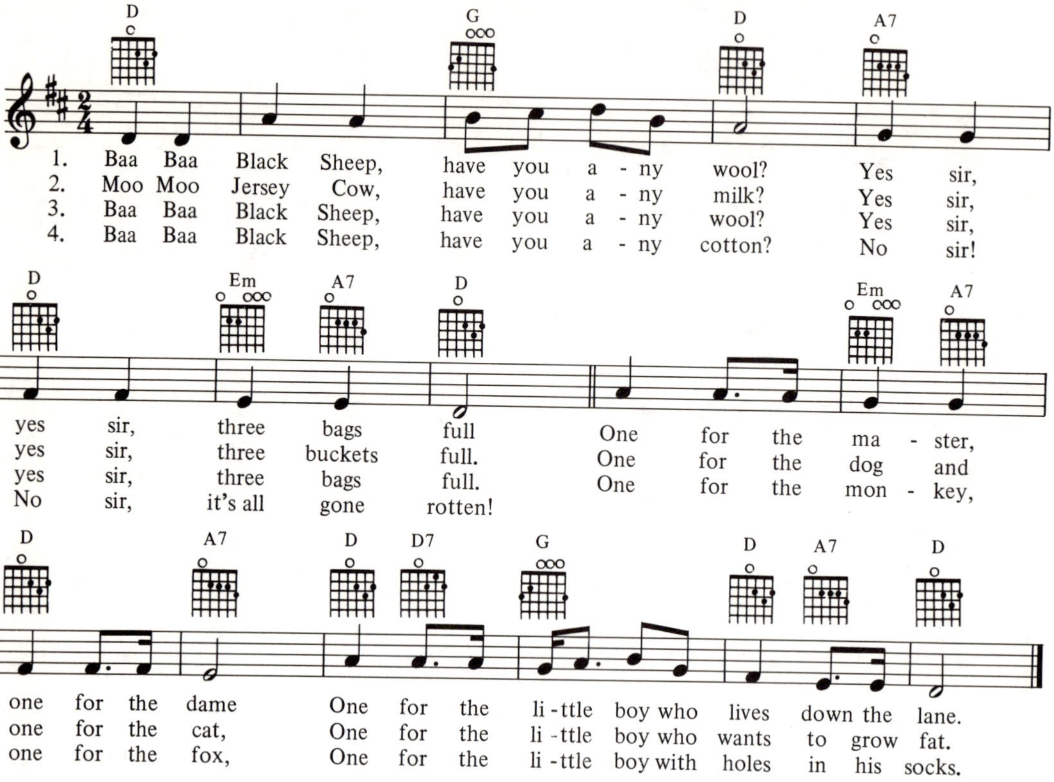

D G D A7 D Em A7 D Em A7 D A7 D D7 G D A7 D

1. Baa Baa Black Sheep, have you a - ny wool? Yes sir, yes sir, three bags full. One for the ma - ster, one for the dame, One for the li - ttle boy who lives down the lane.
2. Moo Moo Jersey Cow, have you a - ny milk? Yes sir, yes sir, three buckets full. One for the dog and one for the cat, One for the li - ttle boy who wants to grow fat.
3. Baa Baa Black Sheep, have you a - ny wool? Yes sir, yes sir, three bags full. One for the mon - key, one for the fox, One for the li - ttle boy with holes in his socks.
4. Baa Baa Black Sheep, have you a - ny cotton? No sir! No sir, it's all gone rotten!

5
Baby Bumble Bee

Traditional/Arranged by Mike Jackson

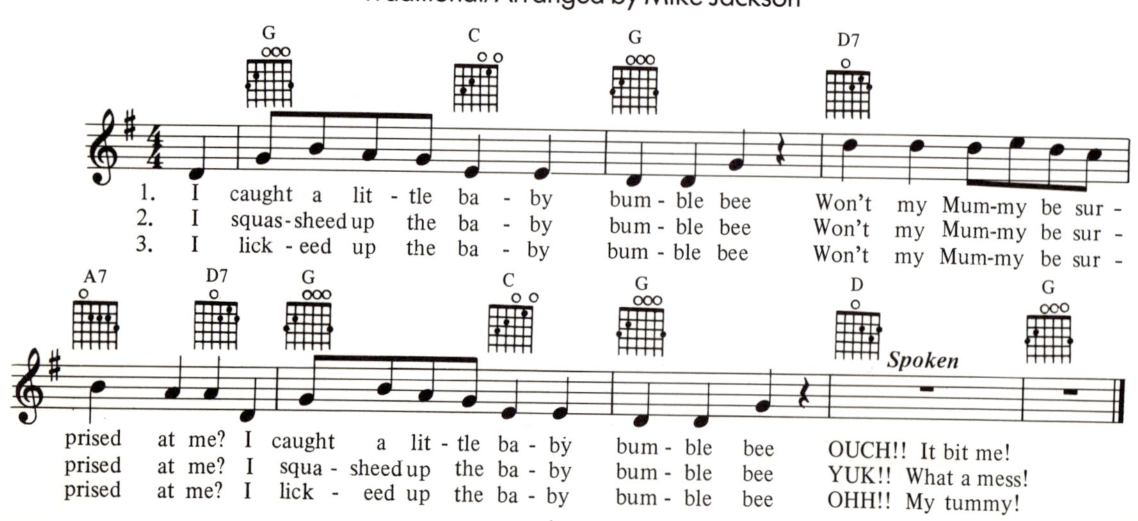
G C G D7 A7 D7 G C G D G
Spoken
1. I caught a lit - tle ba - by bum - ble bee Won't my Mum-my be sur - prised at me? I caught a lit - tle ba - by bum - ble bee OUCH!! It bit me!
2. I squas - sheed up the ba - by bum - ble bee Won't my Mum-my be sur - prised at me? I squa - sheed up the ba - by bum - ble bee YUK!! What a mess!
3. I lick - eed up the ba - by bum - ble bee Won't my Mum-my be sur - prised at me? I lick - eed up the ba - by bum - ble bee OHH!! My tummy!

6
Bananas In Pyjamas

Words & Music by Carey Blyton

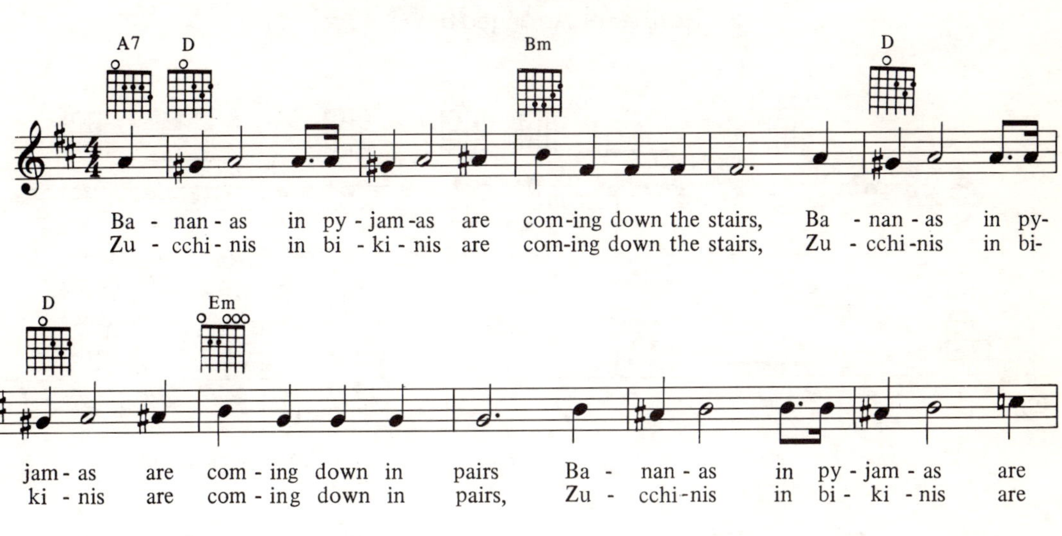
A7 D Bm D
Ba - nan - as in py - jam -as are com-ing down the stairs, Ba - nan - as in py-
Zu - cchi - nis in bi - ki - nis are com-ing down the stairs, Zu - cchi -nis in bi-
D Em
jam - as are com - ing down in pairs Ba - nan - as in py - jam - as are
ki - nis are com - ing down in pairs, Zu - cchi -nis in bi - ki - nis are

A7 D
cha -sing Ted -dy Bears, 'Cos, on Tues-days they all try to catch them un- a - wares.
cha- sing Ted - dy Bears, 'Cos on Tues-days they all try to catch them un -a - wares.

7
The Bear Went Over The Mountain

Traditional/Arranged by Mike Jackson

G C G D G
The bear went ov- er the moun - tain, the bear went o - ver the moun - tain, the
G C G D G
bear went o - ver the moun - tain, to see what he could see. And
G C G C G D
all that he could see, and all that he could see, was the
G C G D G
oth - er side of the moun - tain the oth - er side of the moun - tain, the
G C G D G
oth - er side of the moun - tain, was all that he could see!

8
Bedtime Blues

Words & Music by Mike & Michelle Jackson

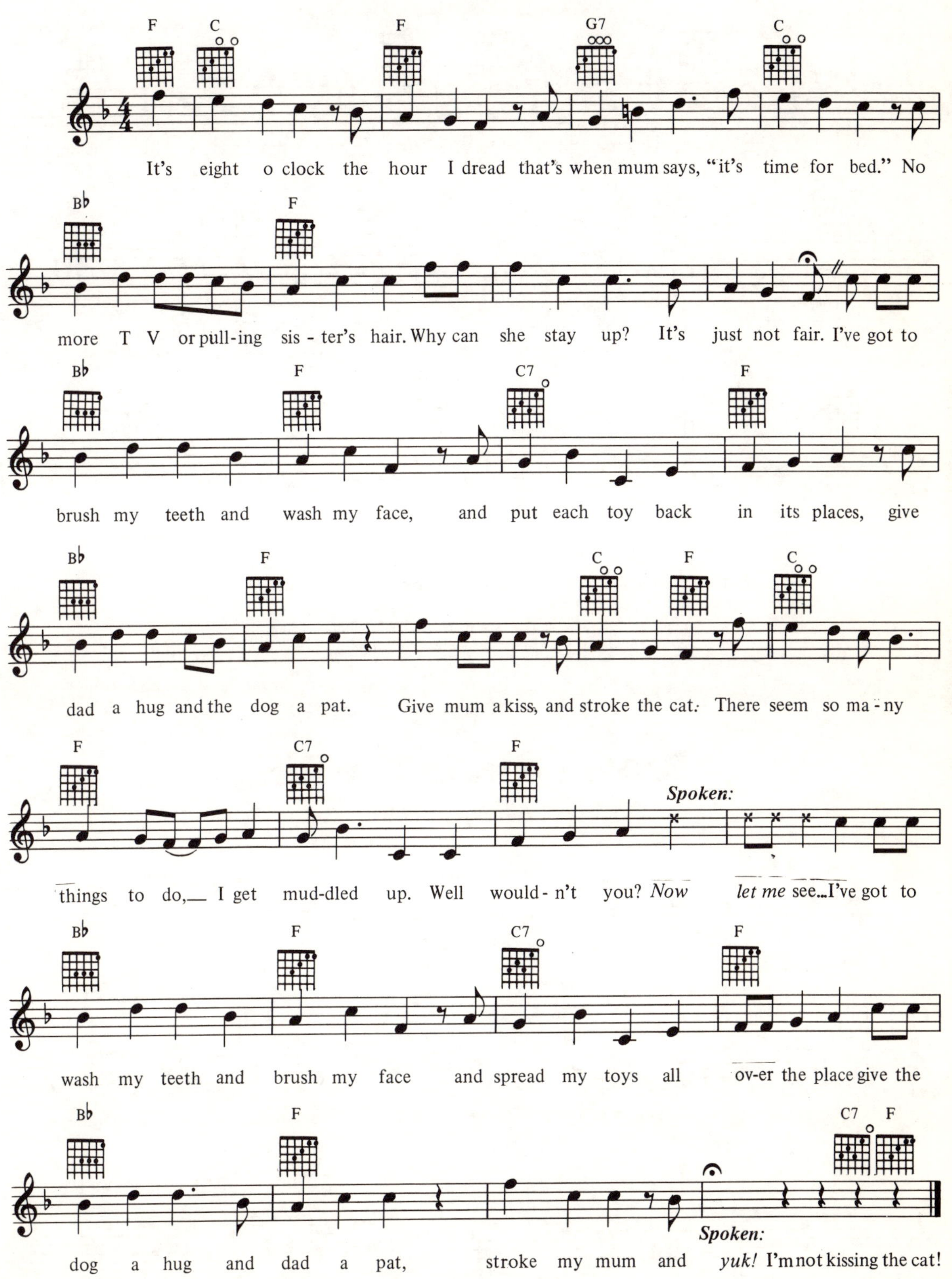
F C F G7 C
It's eight o clock the hour I dread that's when mum says, "it's time for bed." No
B♭ F
more T V or pull-ing sis - ter's hair. Why can she stay up? It's just not fair. I've got to
B♭ F C7 F
brush my teeth and wash my face, and put each toy back in its places, give
B♭ F C F C
dad a hug and the dog a pat. Give mum a kiss, and stroke the cat. There seem so ma - ny
F C7 F
Spoken:
things to do,— I get mud-dled up. Well would - n't you? Now let me see...I've got to
B♭ F C7 F
wash my teeth and brush my face and spread my toys all ov-er the place give the
B♭ F C7 F
dog a hug and dad a pat, stroke my mum and
Spoken:
yuk! I'm not kissing the cat!

9
Bingo

Traditional/Arranged by Mike Jackson

A D A E A

Oh how I love my lit - tle dog and Bin - go is his name.

A D E A

B - I { 1. N - G - O, B - I - N - G - O,
2. N - G (clap), B - I - N - G (clap),
3. N (clap clap), B - I - N (clap clap)

F#m Bm E A

B - I - N - G - O
B - I - N - G (clap)
B - I - N (clap clap) } Bin - go is his name.

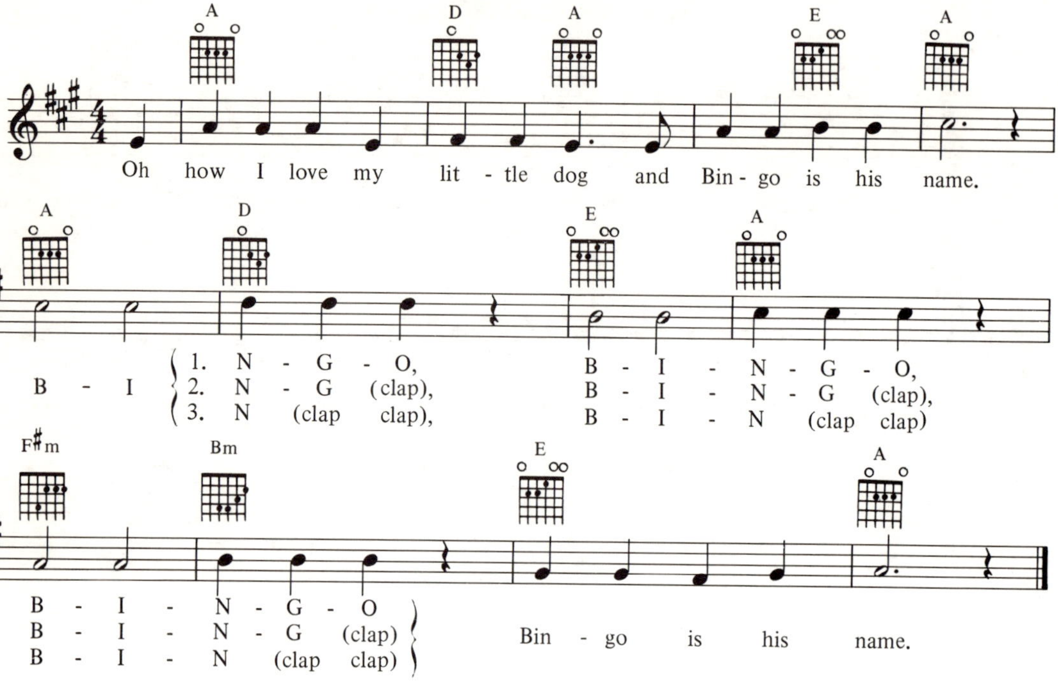

(Repeat, replacing one letter by claps each time.)

10
Brown Girl In The Ring

Traditional/Arranged by Mike Jackson

F
There's a brown girl in the ring tra la - la - la la,
C C7 F
brown girl in the ring tra - la la la la la brown girl in the ring
F C7 F
tra la la la la, she likes sug - ar, I like plum, plum plum!

11
Bondi Tram

Words & Music by Mike & Michelle Jackson

D A7 D
1. Bump-ing down the road on a Bon - di Tram, I look out of the win - dow to
2. Bump-ing down the road on a Bon - di tram, With a spade and buc - ket
3. Bump-ing down the hill on a Bon - di tram, Oh, this hill is steep, mum,
4. Bump-ing to a halt on a Bon - di tram, Race to be first down
G D G A7
see where I am All the pre - tty shops go flash - ing by, I'm
in my hand I'm going to build a cas - tle way up high, the
hold my hand The dri - ver winds the brake on, down we fly way
to the sand Di - g, di - g, dig, pile the sand up high Build the
D G D A7 D
Chorus:
G
rid - ing on a tram down to Bon - di.
best sand - cas - tle at Bon - di.
down the steep hill to Bon - di.
best sand - cas - tle at Bon - di.
Bump - ing Bounc - ing
A7 D G D A7
on a trip to Bon - di, Bump - ing Bounc - ing ri - ding down the road
D G A7 D G D A7 D
Bump - ing Bounc - ing on a trip to Bon - di Ri-ding down the road on a Bon- di Tram.

12
Brumby Jack

Words & Music by Alex Hood

D G D G D A13 A7
1. See the dust cloud on the plain Hear the sound like fall - ing rain
2. There's Stum - py, Bil - ly, Sil - ver Dan, Pick - les, Jim and Pel - i - can He
3. He loves his wild bush friends so well, Many a farm-ing man can tell He'll
4. From the moun - tain side to the dist - ant plain, Here and there and back a - gain They
D G D G D A7 D
Flash - ing hooves and heads held high As the wild bush brum - bies gall - op by.
has a name for ever - y one And when he calls they come at a run.
nev - er eat or go to bed Till he's sure they've all been fed.
roam the count - ry wild and free 'Cause that's the way they want to be.
D G D G D A7
Here comes Brum - by Jack Bring - ing the hor - ses down the track
D G D G D A7 D
Hear him sing as he wheels them a-round He keeps them to-geth - er safe and sound

13
Bunyip In My Watertank

Words & Music by Mike & Michelle Jackson

Dm C Dm

Bun-yip in my wat-er tank, wat-er tank, wat-er tank Bun-yip in my wat-er tank, what

Dm C Dm

do you do all day? — I sit and squi-ggle, I sit and wri-ggle Cause I

C Dm

ate a worm and it's in my mid-dle I'm a bun-yip in your

1. C Dm 2. A7 Dm

wat-er tank That's what I do all day. — I wat-er tank that's what I do all day.

14

The Cat Came Back

Words & Music by Harry S. Miller

Em D C Bm
1. Now old Mr John - son had trou - bles of his own, He
2. On the tel - e-graph wire birds were sit - ting in a bunch. The
3. Well they threw him in the kennel where the dog was fast a- sleep And The
Em D Em Bm Em D
had an old cat and it would - n't leave his. home. He tried all he knew just to
cat licked his lips and said he'd have them for his lunch. He climbed softly to the top and
bones of other cats all lay piled in a heap. Well the ken-nel burst a - part
Em Am Bm B
Chorus
keep the cat a - way He took it up to Ca - na - da and told it for to stay
put his foot upon the wire Well his fur got scorched and his tail caught fire
and the poor dog flew outside With his ears chewed off and holes in his hide
But the
Em D Em D Em D
cat came back, the ver - y next day, the cat came back. They
Em D Em D C Bm Em
thought it was a 'goner' but the cat came back, it just couldn't stay a - way. MEOW!

15
Daddy Fox

Traditional/Arranged by Mike Jackson

G
C
1. Dad - dy Fox went out on a chil - ly night with a ling - tong dil - ly - dong
2. Well, he ran till he came to a great big pen with a ling - tong dil - ly - dong
3. He grabbed the grey goose by the neck with a ling - tong dil - ly - dong
D
kye - ro me And he prayed for the moon to give him light with a
kye - ro me And the ducks and the geese were kept there - in with a
kye - ro me And up with the little ones over his back with a
ling - tong dil - ly - dong kye - ro me
Chorus:
Hey! fa - la - le, fa - la - la, fa - la - lay - ro Hey! fa - la - lay - ro, lay - ro - lee
D7
up jumps John, ring-ing on his bell with a ling - tong dil - ly - dong kye - ro - me.

4. Old Mother Flipper-Flopper jumped out of bed
With a ling-tong dilly-dong kye-ro me
Out of the window she stuck her little head
With a ling-tong dilly-dong kye-ro me.

5. John, he ran to the top of the hill. . .
And he blew his little horn both loud and shrill. . .

6. The fox, he ran to his cosy den. . .
And there were the little ones, eight, nine, ten. . .

7. Then the fox and his wife, without any strife. . .
They cut up the goose with a carving knife. . . .

16

Did You Ever See A Lassie

Traditional/Arranged by Mike Jackson

G
D
1. Did you e - ver see a las - sie go this way and
2. Oh, you can't put your muck in our dust - bin, in our dust - bin, in

G
that way, did you e - ver see a - las - sie go
our dust - bin you can't put your muck in our dust - bin 'cause

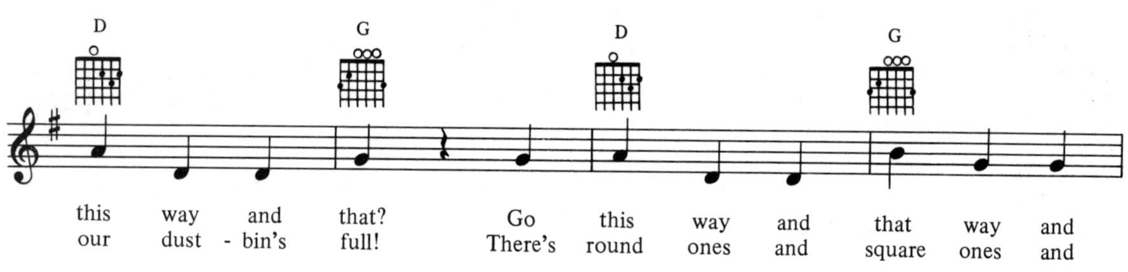

D
G
D
G
this way and that? Go this way and that way and
our dust - bin's full! There's round ones and square ones and

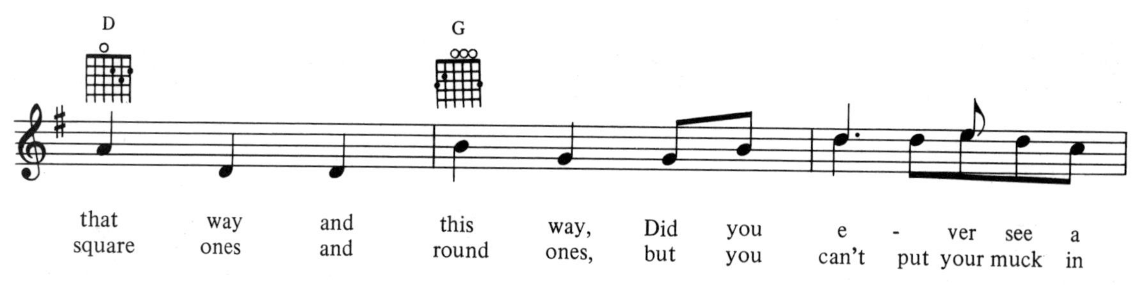

D
G
that way and this way, Did you e - ver see a
square ones and round ones, but you can't put your muck in

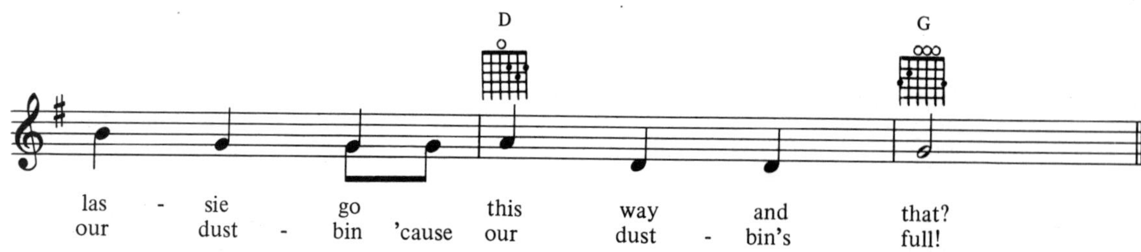

D
G
las - sie go this way and that?
our dust - bin 'cause our dust - bin's full!

17
Down By The Bay

Words: Traditional/Verses 2 & 3 Adapted by Mike Jackson
Music: Traditional/Arranged by Mike Jackson

F7
B♭
Down by the 1) bay (down by the bay) where the wat - er - mel - ons
2) sea (down by the sea) where the lit - tle fish - ies
3) lake (down by the lake) where the wat - er birds
F
F7
grow (where the wat-er mel-ons grow) Back to my home(back to my home) I dare not
grow (where the wat-er fish-ies grow) Back to my home
grow (where the wat-er birds grow) Back to my home
B♭
B♭7
E♭
go (I dare not go) For if I did (for if I
E♭
B♭
did) My moth - er would say (my moth - er would say) Did you
B♭
1) Ev - er see a goose do a hu - la with a noose?
2) Ev - er see a horse do a Ha - ka in the gorse
3) Ev - er see a snake rock 'n' rol - ling in the lake
1.2.
3.
F7
B♭
F7
B♭
down where the wat - er - mel - ons grow down by the grow
down where the lit - tle - fish - ies grow down by the
down where the wat - er birds grow down by the

18
Down To The Sea In Boats

Written by Vincent B. Brophy/Arranged by Mike Jackson

Lively
C F C F C
Chorus: Let's go down to the sea in boats, for I'm a sail - or on the sea!
C F G C
Let's go down to the sea, and see what we can see!
C G/B Am F Em Dm G
1. Dressed in our Sun - day best we'll ride, o - ver the dus - ty, bump - ity road,
2. Clippers and col - liers by the sea, oh what a treat for you and me,
3. Punch and Ju - dy by the sea, a live - ly show and all for free,
C Dm Em Am C
Down to the Bel- - more Bas - in ti - de neck to knees are
Life on the waves, you'll have to be bra - ve when you go to the
From Mar- ket Square the band it pla - ys jigs and reels to a
G C
all the rage!
sea in boats.
live - ly sway.

4. The collier lads from up the mine are sending coal by railway line.
The boats are berthed, the trimmers engaged, all working in the colony's trade.

5. Far away and raising steam, the colliers chug with bellies of coal,
From Brighton Hotel it's a lively scene, when you go to the sea in boats.

6. The tallyman tallies the tons of coal,
the steamer Undolla's filled her holds,
The whistle blows, she's under tow when you go to the sea in boats.

19
Found A Peanut

Traditional/Arranged by Mike Jackson

G
D
C
G
D
G
1. Found a pea - nut, found a pea - nut, found a
2. Where'd you find it, where'd you find it, where'd you
pea - nut last___ night, last___ night I found a
find it last___ night, last___ night___ where'd you
pea - nut, found a pea - nut, last___ night.
find it, where'd you find it last___ night.

In a dustbin. . .

Cracked it open. . .

Found it rotten. . .

Ate it anyway. . .

I felt sick. . .

Called the doctor. . .

Went to Heaven. . .

Didn't want me. . .

Went the other way. . . (thumbs down)

Shovelling coal. . .

Found a peanut. . .

(St. Patrick's, School, Nanango, Qld.)

20
Frère Jacques

Words: Traditional
Music: Traditional/Arranged by Mike & Michelle Jackson

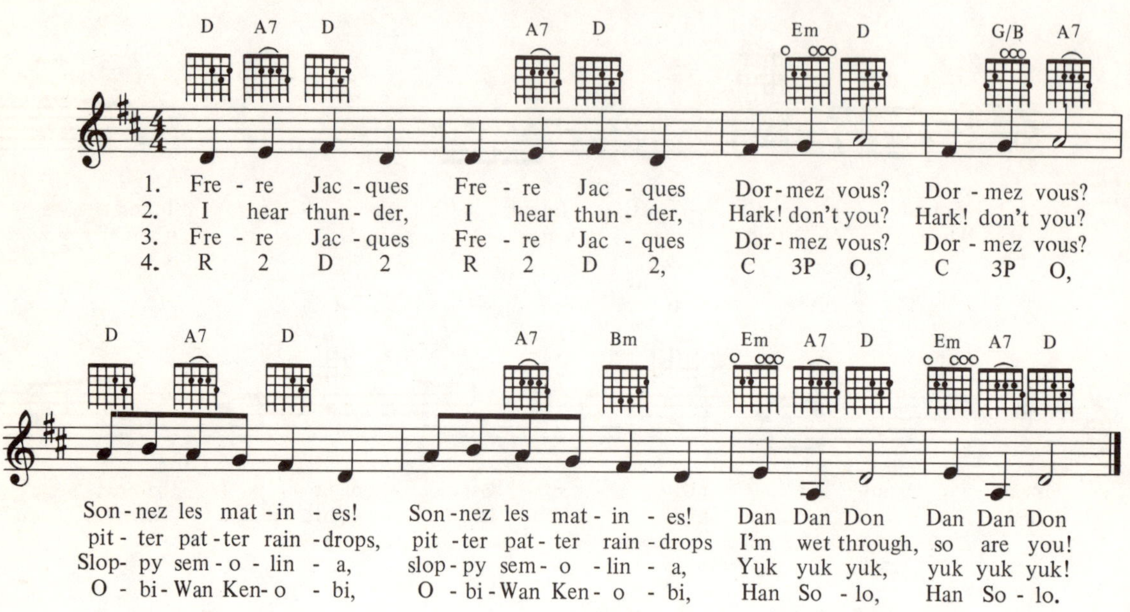
D A7 D A7 D Em D G/B A7
D A7 D A7 Bm Em A7 D Em A7 D
1. Fre - re Jac - ques Fre - re Jac - ques Dor - mez vous? Dor - mez vous?
2. I hear thun - der, I hear thun - der, Hark! don't you? Hark! don't you?
3. Fre - re Jac - ques Fre - re Jac - ques Dor - mez vous? Dor - mez vous?
4. R 2 D 2 R 2 D 2, C 3P O, C 3P O,
Son - nez les mat - in - es! Son - nez les mat - in - es! Dan Dan Don Dan Dan Don
pit - ter pat - ter rain - drops, pit - ter pat - ter rain - drops I'm wet through, so are you!
Slop - py sem - o - lin - a, slop - py sem - o - lin - a, Yuk yuk yuk, yuk yuk yuk!
O - bi - Wan Ken - o - bi, O - bi - Wan Ken - o - bi, Han So - lo, Han So - lo.

SEMOLINA

21
Frog Went A-Courting

Traditional/Arranged by Mike Jackson

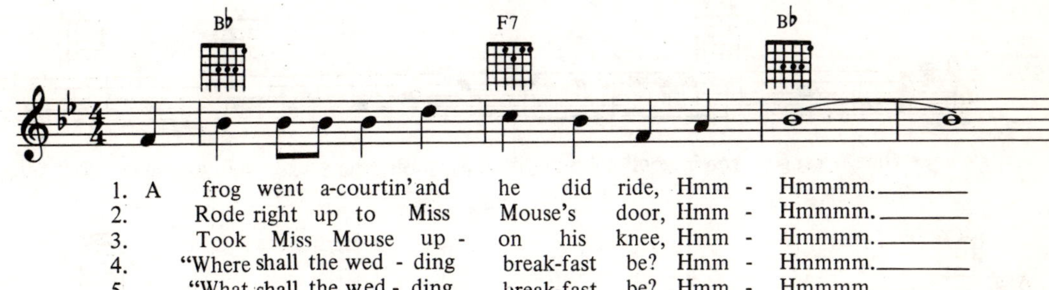
B♭
F7
B♭
1. A frog went a-courtin' and he did ride, Hmm - Hmmmm.
2. Rode right up to Miss Mouse's door, Hmm - Hmmmm.
3. Took Miss Mouse up - on his knee, Hmm - Hmmmm.
4. "Where shall the wed - ding break-fast be? Hmm - Hmmmm.
5. "What shall the wed - ding break-fast be? Hmm - Hmmmm.

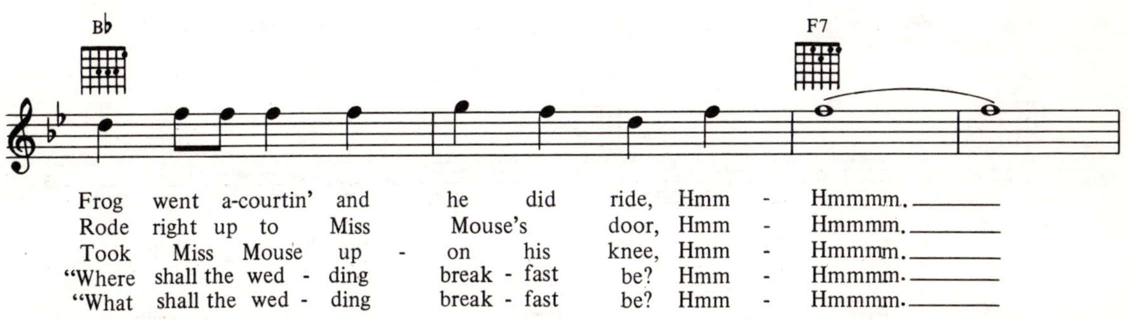
B♭
F7
Frog went a-courtin' and he did ride, Hmm - Hmmmm.
Rode right up to Miss Mouse's door, Hmm - Hmmmm.
Took Miss Mouse up - on his knee, Hmm - Hmmmm.
"Where shall the wed - ding break - fast be? Hmm - Hmmmm.
"What shall the wed - ding break - fast be? Hmm - Hmmmm.

B♭
B♭7
E♭

Frog went a-courtin' and he did ride, with a Sword and a pis - tol
Rode right up to Miss Mouse's door, Gave three raps and
Took Miss Mouse up - on his knee, Said, "Miss Mouse, will you
"Where shall the wed - ding break - fast be?" "Down in the swamp in the
"What shall the wed - ding break - fast be?" "Fried mos - quito and a

B♭
F
B♭
by his side, Hmm - Hmmmm, Hmm - Hmmmm, Hmm - Hmmmm.
a very loud roar, Hmm - Hmmmm, Hmm - Hmmmm, Hmm - Hmmmm.
mar - ry me?" Hmm - Hmmmm, Hmm - Hmmmm, Hmm - Hmmmm.
hol - low tree." Hmm - Hmmmm, Hmm - Hmmmm, Hmm - Hmmmm.
black - eyed pea." Hmm - Hmmmm, Hmm - Hmmmm, Hmm - Hmmmm.

22
Ging Gang Goolie

Traditional/Arranged by Mike Jackson

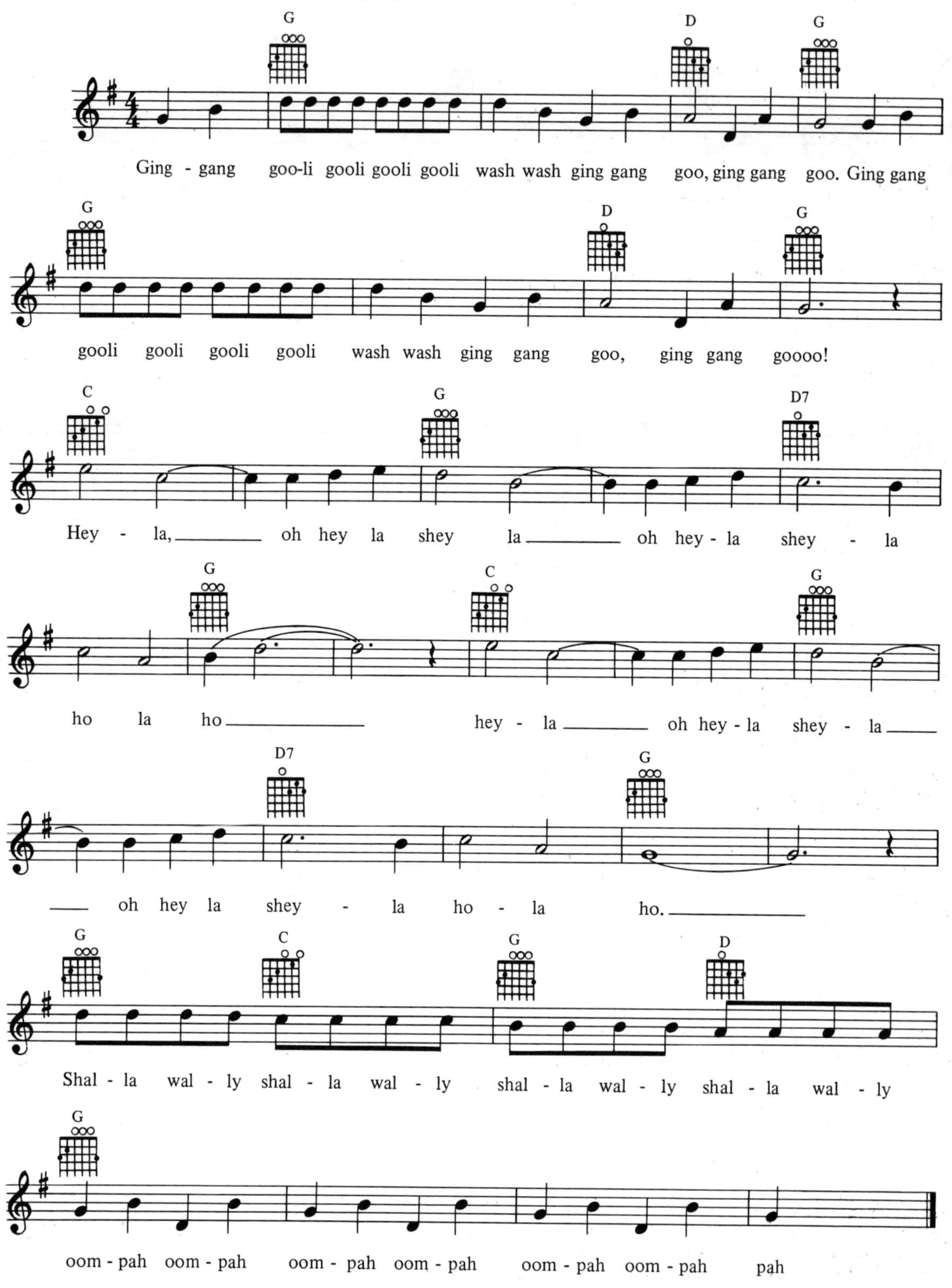
G
D
G
Ging - gang goo-li gooli gooli gooli wash wash ging gang goo, ging gang goo. Ging gang
G
D
G
gooli gooli gooli gooli wash wash ging gang goo, ging gang goooo!
C
G
D7
Hey - la, oh hey la shey la oh hey - la shey - la
G
C
G
ho la ho hey - la oh hey - la shey - la
D7
G
oh hey la shey - la ho - la ho.
G
C
G
D
Shal - la wal - ly shal - la wal - ly shal - la wal - ly shal - la wal - ly
G
oom - pah oom - pah oom - pah oom - pah oom - pah oom - pah pah

23
Going Over The Sea

Words: Traditional/Adapted by Mike Jackson
Music: Traditional/Arranged by Mike Jackson

G
D
G
1. When I was one I played a drum,
2. When I was two I played a ka-zoo,
3. When I was three I sang mer-ri-ly,
4. When I was four I danced on the floor,
5. When I was five I did a jive,
Go-ing ov-er the sea. I
jumped a-board a pi-rate's ship and the cap-tain said — to me, We're go-ing
Chorus
this way that way for-wards and back-wards ov-er the Ir-ish sea. We're go-ing
this way that way for-wards and back-wards ov-er the Ir-ish sea.

24
Gravity

Words & Music by Jan Holdstock

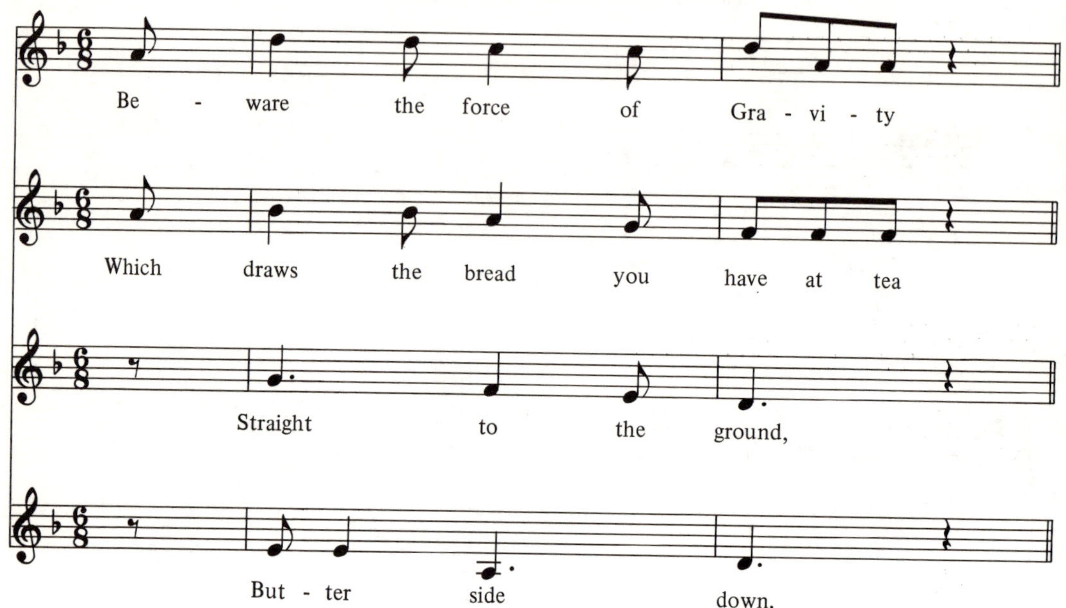
Be - ware the force of Gra - vi - ty
Which draws the bread you have at tea
Straight to the ground,
But - ter side down.

25
Great Tom

Traditional/Arranged by Mike Jackson

Great Tom is cast, and
Christ church bells ring "One, two, three, four, five,
six." And Tom comes last.

26
Happy Birthday

By M. & P. Hill

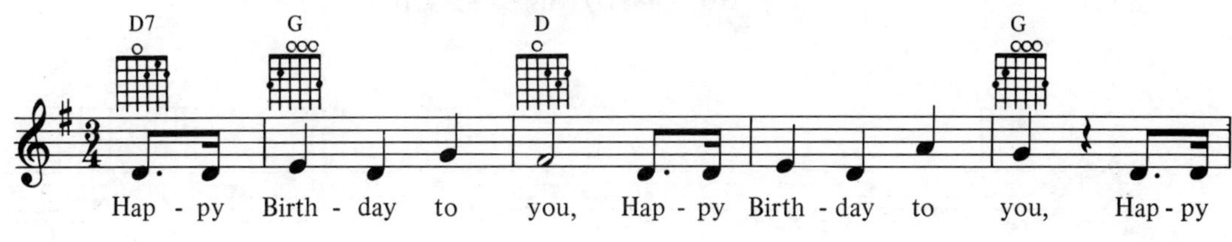
D7
G
D
G
Hap - py Birth - day to you, Hap - py Birth - day to you, Hap - py

G7
C
G
D
G
Birth - day dear ( ) Hap - py Birth - day to you

27
Happy Moron

Traditional/Arranged by Mike Jackson

1. There goes a hap - py mor - on.

2. He does - n't give a damn! I

3. wish ___ I ___ were a ___ mor - on, Oh

4. Crumbs! per - haps I am!

#28
Hark The Herald Angels Sing

Words & Music by C. Wesley/G. Whitfield & M. Madan
Arranged by Mike Jackson

G D G Am G D G
1. Hark! the he - rald ang - els sing___ Glo - ry to the new- born King;
2. Christ, by high - est heaven a - dored___ Christ, the ev - er last - ing Lord,
3. Hail the heaven - born Prince of Peace!___ Hail the sun of Right-eous-ness!
G A7 D A D A D7
Peace on earth mer - cy mild,___ God and sin - ners re - con- ciled:
Late in time be - hold him come___ Off - spring of the Vir - gin's womb;
Light and life to all he brings,___ Risen with heal - ing in his wings:
G D G D G D7 G D
Joy - ful all ye nat - ions rise,___ Join the tri - umph of the skies,___
Veiled in flesh the God- head see;___ Hail the in-car- nate De - it - y!___
Mild he lays his glo - ry by,___ Born that man no more may die,___
C Am D7 G
With the an-gel - ic host pro - claim, Christ is___born in Beth - le - hem:
Pleased as man with man to dwell, Jes - us___our Em - man - u - el:
Born to raise the sons of earth, Born to___give them sec - ond birth:
C Am D G D G
Hark! the he - rald ang - els sing Glo - ry___ to the new - born king.

29

Hi, Hi, The Little Boat Rides

Written by Vincent P. Brophy/Arranged by Mike Jackson

Chorus

Em
D
Hi, hi the lit-tle boat rides, on the o-cean broad and wide.

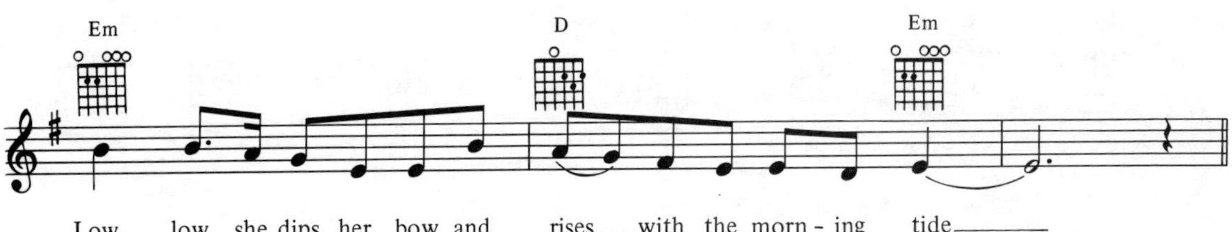
Em
D
Em
Low, low she dips her bow and rises___ with the morn-ing tide_______

Em
Bm7
Em
Bm7

1. Three white masts the sail - maker made, ev - ery stitch to hold its grade, the
2. Our little ship is stout and strong, through all weather she'll sail a - long, the

Em Bm7 Em D Em

wind may blow and the rain may fall, but nev-er an inch will give her way_______
rig-ging's full and the ropes are tight,___ maybe we'll sail the Australian Bight_____

3. Bright and early, all hands on board, scrub the decks, or by the Lord. . . !
The bosun cries "Bend yer backs!" Scrub-a-dub-dub, all clean and white.
Chorus:
4. There's many an hour we'll spend below, old hands will tell of days long ago,
Seafaring days, stories long - by the light of a hurricane lamp.
Chorus:
5. The look-out cries "There's land a-ho!" - a joyful shout from the crew below,
Sea breeze is up, we're closer now, sail to port with our masts so proud!

30
Humpty Dumpty

Traditional/Arranged by Mike Jackson

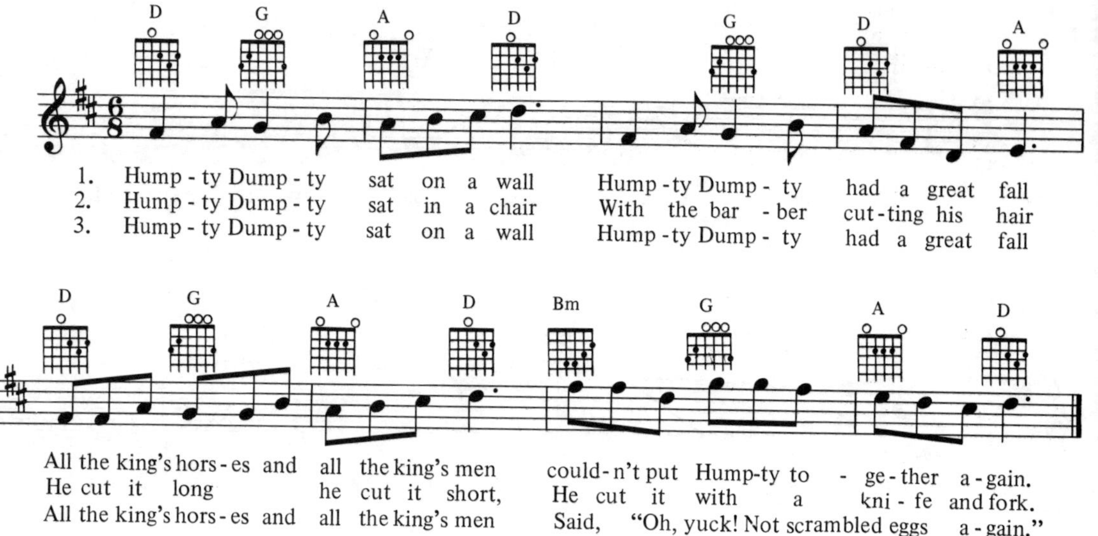
D G A D G D A
1. Hump - ty Dump - ty sat on a wall Hump - ty Dump - ty had a great fall
2. Hump - ty Dump - ty sat in a chair With the bar - ber cut - ting his hair
3. Hump - ty Dump - ty sat on a wall Hump - ty Dump - ty had a great fall
D G A D Bm G A D
All the king's hors - es and all the king's men could - n't put Hump-ty to - ge - ther a - gain.
He cut it long he cut it short, He cut it with a kni - fe and fork.
All the king's hors - es and all the king's men Said, "Oh, yuck! Not scrambled eggs a - gain."

31
I Know An Old Lady Who Swallowed A Fly

Traditional/Arranged by Mike Jackson

C
D7
I know an old la - dy who swall-owed a fly, I don't know why she
G
G7
C
swall - owed a fly per - haps she'll die!
C
D7
I know an old la - dy who swall-owed a spid - er that wrig-gled and jig - gled and
Repeat as necessary
G7
C
tickl - ed in - side her. She swall - owed the spid - er to catch the fly,
D7
G
G7
C
I don't know why she swall-owed the fly, per-haps she'll die!

3. I know an old lady who swallowed a bird.
   How absurd, to swallow a bird!
   She swallowed the bird to catch the spider
   That wriggled. . . . etc.

4. I know an old lady who swallowed a cat,
   Just fancy that, she swallowed a cat!
   She swallowed the cat to catch the bird,
   She swallowed the bird to catch the spider
   That wriggled. . . . etc.

5. I know an old lady who swallowed a dog,
   What a hog, to swallow a dog!
   She swallowed the dog to catch the cat,
   She swallowed the cat. . . . etc.

6. I know an old lady who swallowed a goat.
   She just opened her throat and swallowed a goat!
   She swallowed the goat to catch the dog,
   She swallowed the dog. . . . etc.

7. I know an old lady who swallowed a cow.
   I don't know HOW she swallowed a cow.
   She swallowed the cow to catch the goat,
   She swallowed the goat. . . . etc.

8. I know an old lady who swallowed a rhinoceros,
   THAT'S PREPOSTEROUS! !
   She swallowed the rhino to catch the cow,
   She swallowed the cow. . . . etc.

9. I know an old lady who swallowed a horse.
   She's dead of course.

32

If You're Happy And You Know It

Traditional/Arranged by Mike & Michelle Jackson

4. If you're happy and you know it,
shout hurray - HURRAY
If you're happy and you know it,
shout hurray - HURRAY
If you're happy and you know it,
you really ought to show it
If you're happy and you know it,
shout hurray, stamp your feet,
nod your head, clap your hands.

5. If you're happy and you know it,
clap your hands - CLAP CLAP
If you're happy and you know it,
clap your hands - CLAP CLAP
If you're happy and you know it,
you really ought to show it
If you're happy and you know it,
clap your hands, shout hurray,
stamp your feet, nod your head,
clap your hands.

I'm A Little Teapot

Words & Music in first verse: C. Kelley & G. Saunders.

C
F
C
1. I'm a lit - tle tea - pot, short and stout
2. I'm a tube of tooth - paste on the shelf
3. I'm a lit - tle ro - bot short and square
F
C
G
C
Here is my han - dle, Here is my spout
I get so lone - ly all by my - self
I have no toe - nails, I have no hair
C
F
C
When I get all steamed up, then I shout
when it comes to night - time, then I shout Just
If you want an ans - wer to a sum Just
Am
F
G
C
Tip me o - ver, pour me out.
lift my lid up, squeeze me out.
press the but - ton, out it comes.

34
I'm A Nut

Traditional/Arranged by Mike Jackson

D
1. I'm a lit - tle a - - corn, small and round
2. I love me, I think I'm grand I
3. I call my - self on the tel - e - phone

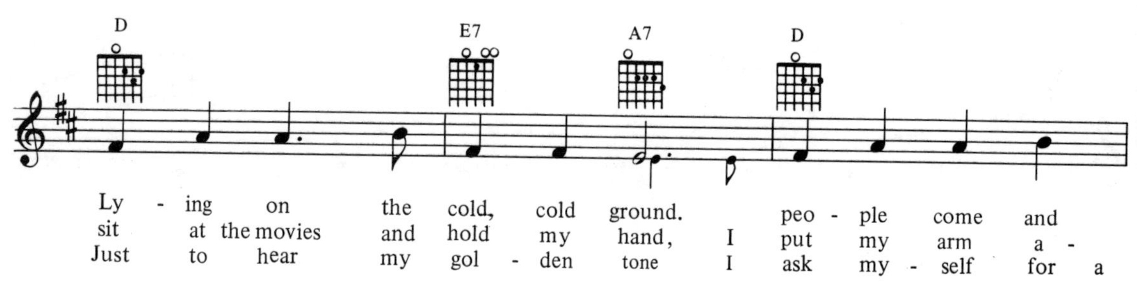
D
E7
A7
D
Ly - ing on the cold, cold ground. peo - ple come and
sit at the movies and hold my hand, I put my arm a -
Just to hear my gol - den tone I ask my - self for a

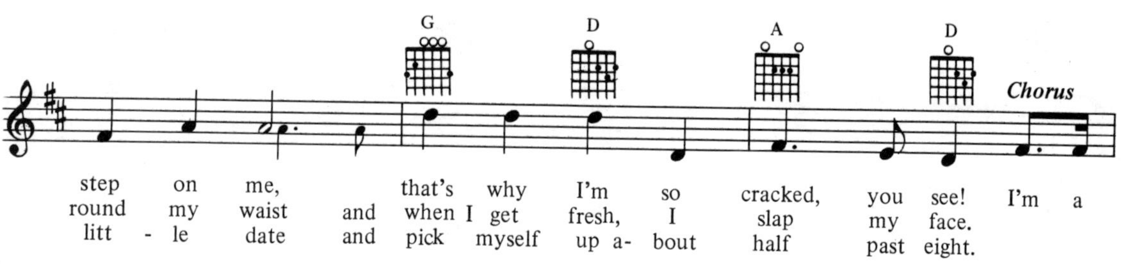
G
D
A
D
Chorus
step on me, that's why I'm so cracked, you see! I'm a
round my waist and when I get fresh, I slap my face.
litt - le date and pick myself up a- bout half past eight.

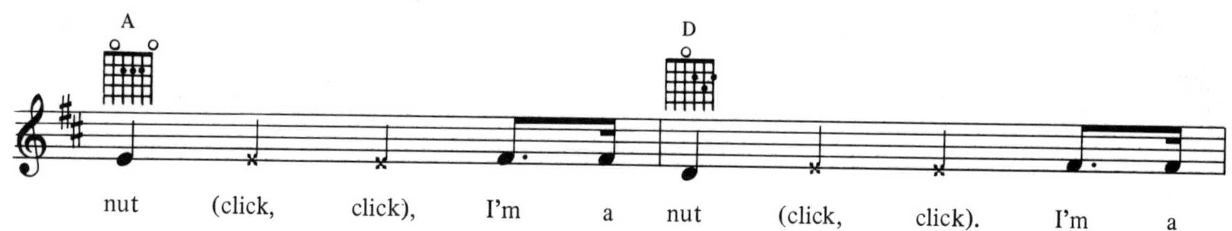
A
D
nut (click, click), I'm a nut (click, click). I'm a

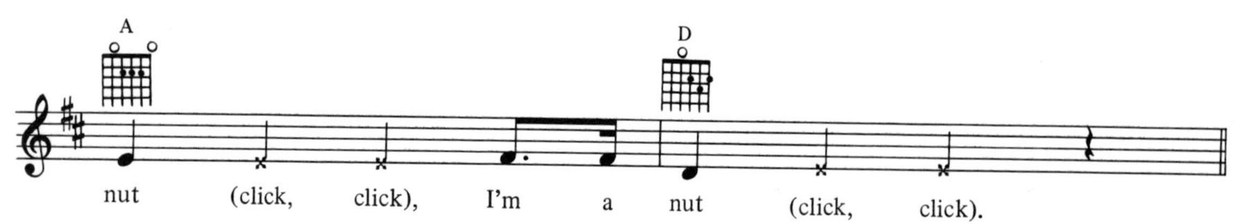
A
D
nut (click, click), I'm a nut (click, click).

35

I'm Gonna Tell

Words & Music by Rosalie Sorrels

D G D

(Chorus) I'm gon-na tell, I'm gon-na tell, I'm gon-na
1. I'm gon-na tell Mum that you hid the broom, so you wouldn't
2. Well I'm gonna tell that you broke a plate, and I'm gon-na
3. I'm gon-na tell that you kicked me and bit me, and I'm gon-na

E A7 D

hol-ler and I'm gon-na yell. I'll get you in trou-ble for
have ___ to sweep up the room. Then Mum would sweep it
tell on all the ba-na-nas you ate. I'll tell on you one time, I'll
tell that you punched me and hit me, But I won't tell Mummy what

Bm A D

ev-ery thing you do, I'm gon-na tell on you.
up for you, I'm gon-na tell on you. (Chorus)
tell on you two, I'm gon-na tell on you. (Chorus)
I ___ did to you, I'm just gon-na tell on you (Chorus)

36
In The Land Of Oz

Traditional/Arranged by Mike Jackson
Collected from the children of Rosebery School, Tasmania

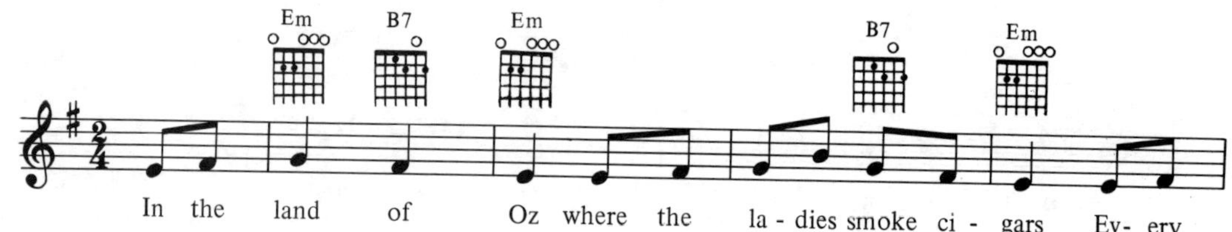
Em
B7
Em
B7
Em
In the land of Oz where the la - dies smoke ci - gars Ev- ery

Em
B7
Em
B7
Em
puff they make is e - nough to kill a snake And when the

Em
B7
Em
B7
Em
snakes are dead they put ros - es round their head And when the
ros - es die they put dia - monds in their eyes And when the
dia - monds break then it's Nine - teen Eigh - ty Eight!

(This is a clapping game. Two people clapping their partner's hands to the rhythm of the song. On the word "Eight" both partners "freeze" and the first one to move is out.)

37
I Was Only Fooling

Words: Verse 1 Traditional
Verses 2 & 3 Mike Jackson
Music: Traditional/Arranged by Mike Jackson

A
A7
1. I wear my silk py-jam - as in the sum-mer when it's hot, I
2. I jumped in - to a sub - ma - rine and flew up to the moon, Made
3. Our fa - ther had a car that went much slo - wer than he planned. 'Cos
D
A
wear my flan - nel night - ie in the win - ter when it's not But
cheese and pic - kle sand - wich - es and got back home by noon, Then I
he'd ex-changed the eng - ine for a gi - ant rub - ber band He
A
F♯m
some - times in the spring - time and some - times in the fall, I
sailed a Jum - bo Jet three days and nights on stor - my seas Till I
wound the band so tight - ly that it gave a groan and snapped And it
D
E7
A
slip be - tween the co - vers with no - thing on at all!
found a hip - po - pot - a - mus who coun - ted up to three!
took us se - ven weeks to get our poor old Dad un-wrapped!
A
D
A
I was on-ly, on-ly fool - ing, I was on-ly, on-ly fool - ing, I was on-ly, on-ly
F♯m
B7
E7
A
fool - ing 1. A - bout the spring - time and the fall!
2. A - bout the hip - po pot - a - mus who counted up to three!
3. A - bout the sev - ven weeks it took to get poor Dad unwrapped!

I Whistle A Happy Tune

Words by Oscar Hammerstein II
Music by Richard Rodgers

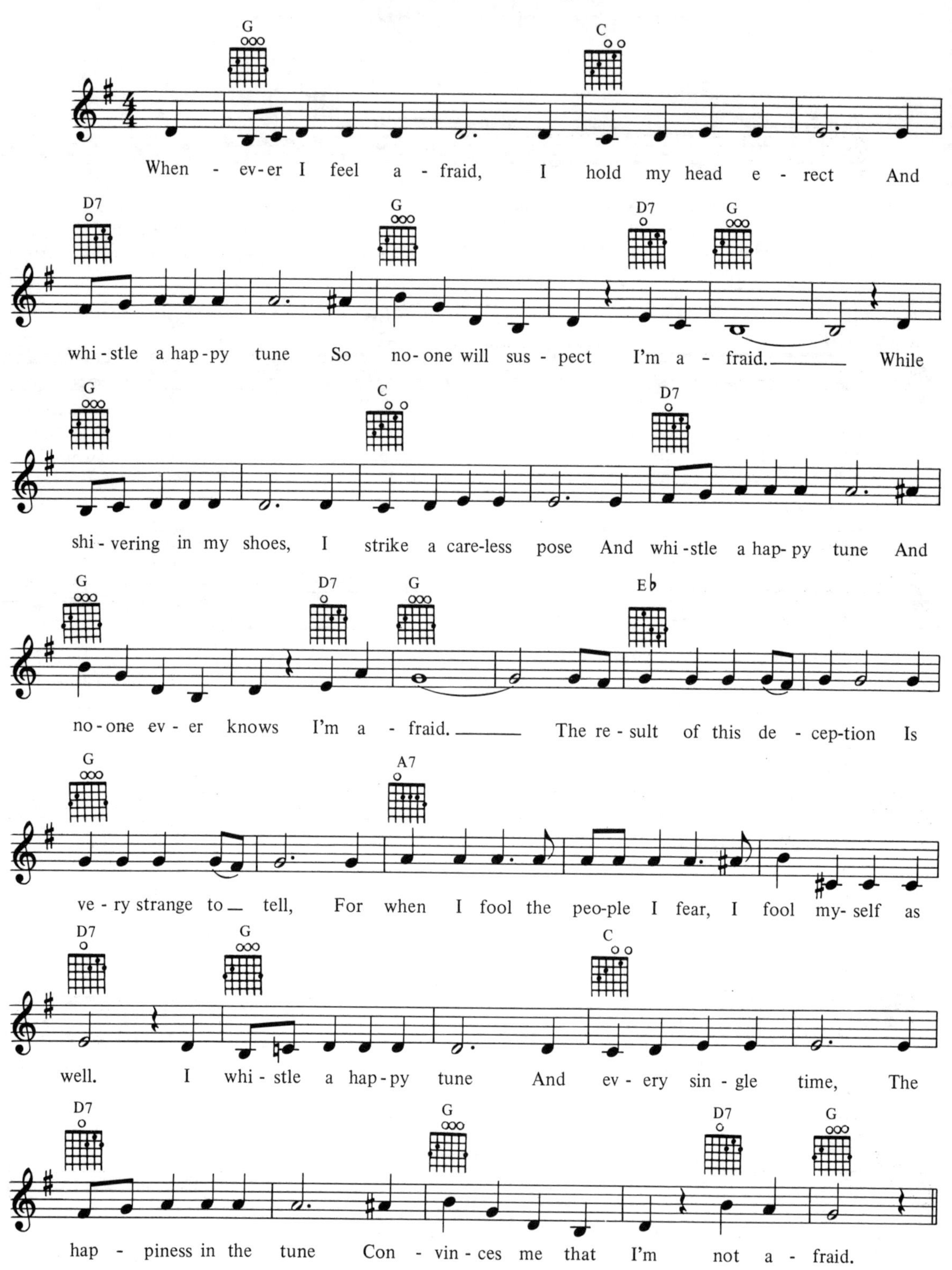
G
C
When - ev-er I feel a - fraid, I hold my head e - rect And
D7
G
D7
G
whi-stle a hap-py tune So no-one will sus - pect I'm a - fraid. While
G
C
D7
shi-vering in my shoes, I strike a care-less pose And whi-stle a hap-py tune And
G
D7
G
E♭
no-one ev - er knows I'm a - fraid. The re - sult of this de - cep-tion Is
G
A7
ve - ry strange to tell, For when I fool the peo-ple I fear, I fool my-self as
D7
G
C
well. I whi - stle a hap-py tune And ev - ery sin - gle time, The
D7
G
D7
G
hap - piness in the tune Con - vin-ces me that I'm not a - fraid.

Jingle Bells

Traditional/Arranged by Mike Jackson

G C G C D7

Jin - gle bells, jin - gle bells, jin - gle all the way. Oh what fun it

G Em 1. A7 D7 2. D7 G

is to ride in a one horse o - pen sleigh. Hey! one horse o - pe n sleigh

G G7 C 1. C D7

Dash - ing through the snow, in a one horse o - pen sleigh, o'er the fields we go

Bells on bob - tails ring ma - king spir - its bright, what

D7 G 2. C D7 G Em Am D7 G

laugh - ing all the way, fun it is to laugh and sing a sleigh - ing song to - night.

40
John Brown's Holden

First Verse: Traditional
Verses 2 & 3: Mike & Michelle Jackson

John Brown's Hol-den's got a punc-ture in a tyre, John Brown's Hol-den's got a
John Brown's pushbike wouldn't pe - dal ve - ry fast, John Brown's pushbike wouldn't
John Brown's speedboat wouldn't start on Sa - tur- day, John Brown's speedboat wouldn't

punc-ture in a tyre, John Brown's Hol den's got a punc-ture in a tyre, So they
pe - dal ve - ry fast, John Brown's push-bike wouldn't pe - dal ver - ry fast, So he
start on Sat - ur-day, John Brown's speed-boat wouldn't start on Sa -tur-day, So he

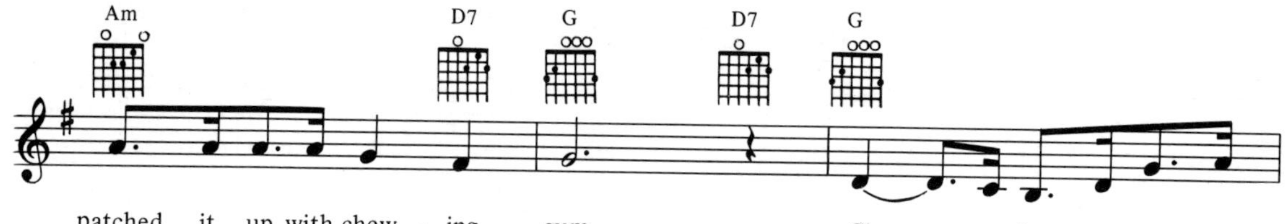

patched it up with chew - ing gum. Chew - y, chew - y, chew - y,
fixed it with the engine from his mower. Now ___ he's try - ing hard to
fixed it with an engine from a plane. Now ___ he's sailed past Hal - ley's

chew - ing gum, Chew - y, chew - y, chew - y, chew - ing gum,
stop ___ it, Now he's try - ing hard to stop ___ it,
Com - et, Now he's sailed past Hal - ley's Com - et,

Chew -y, chew-y, chew-y, chew-ing gum So they patched it up with chew - ing gum.
Now_he's try-ing hard to stop ___ it, Since he fixed it with the engine from his mower.
Now_he's sailed past Halley's Com - et, Will we ev - er see ___ John Brown a-gain?

41
Kangaroos Like To Hop

Words & Music by Leon Rosselson

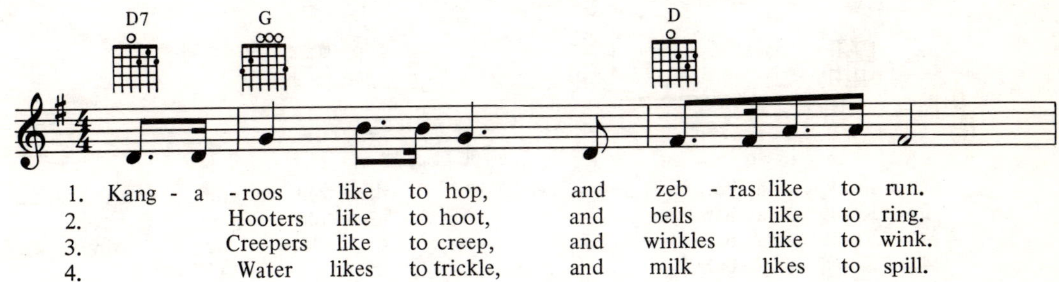
D7
G
D
1. Kang - a - roos like to hop, and zeb - ras like to run.
2. Hooters like to hoot, and bells like to ring.
3. Creepers like to creep, and winkles like to wink.
4. Water likes to trickle, and milk likes to spill.

C
D7
G
Hors - es like to trot, but I like to lie in the sun.
Scoot - ers like to scoot, but I like to swing on a swing.
People like to peep, but I like to splash in the sink.
Glue likes to stickle, but I like to roll down the hill.

5. Feet like to jump, tummies like to hum.
Knees like to bump, but I like to suck my thumb.

6. Panthers like to pounce, and leopards like to leap.
Bulls like to bounce, but I like to sing in my sleep.

7. Kangaroos like to to hop, and zebras like to run.
Horses like to trot, but I like to lie in the sun.

42
Kookaburra Sits

Words & Music in Verse 1: M. Sinclair

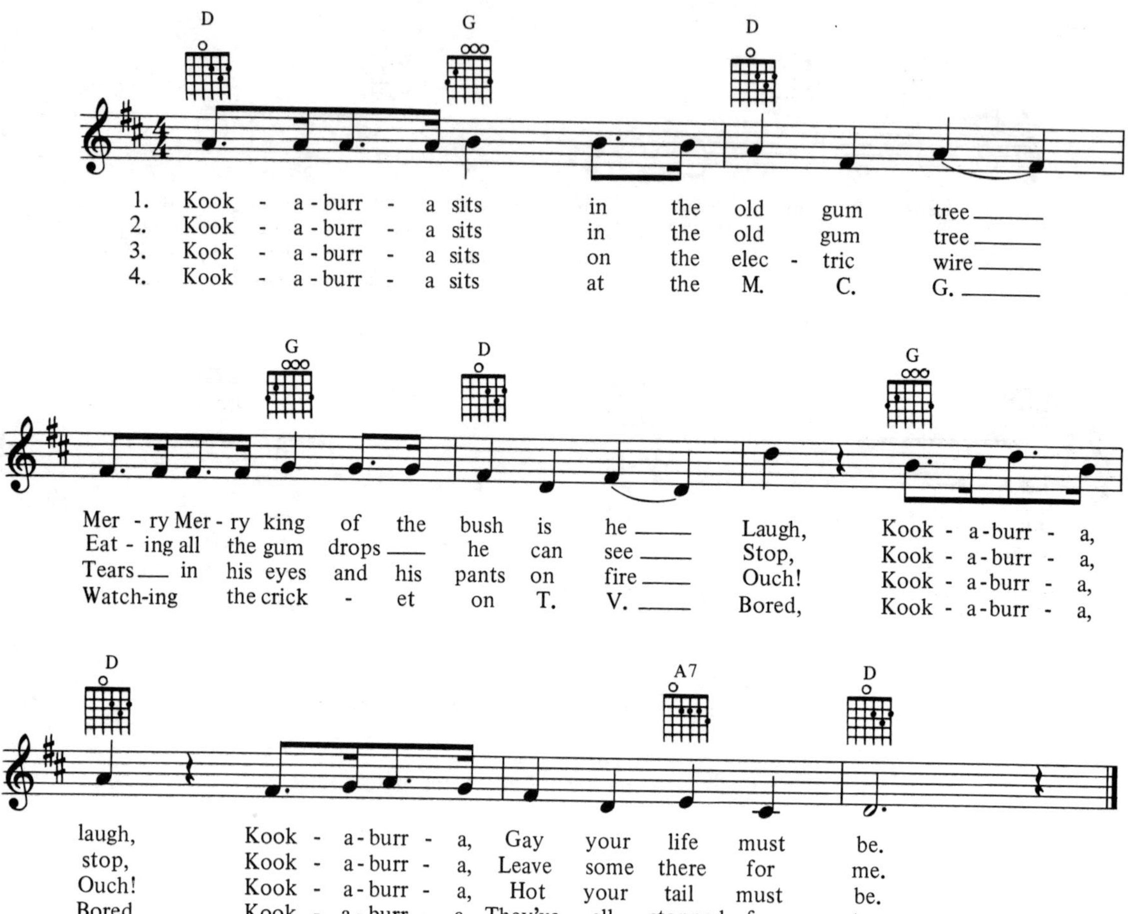
D
G
D
1. Kook - a - burr - a sits in the old gum tree
2. Kook - a - burr - a sits in the old gum tree
3. Kook - a - burr - a sits on the elec - tric wire
4. Kook - a - burr - a sits at the M. C. G.
G
D
G
Mer - ry Mer - ry king of the bush is he Laugh, Kook - a - burr - a,
Eat - ing all the gum drops he can see Stop, Kook - a - burr - a,
Tears in his eyes and his pants on fire Ouch! Kook - a - burr - a,
Watch-ing the crick - et on T. V. Bored, Kook - a - burr - a,
D
A7
D
laugh, Kook - a - burr - a, Gay your life must be.
stop, Kook - a - burr - a, Leave some there for me.
Ouch! Kook - a - burr - a, Hot your tail must be.
Bored, Kook - a - burr - a, They've all stopped for tea.

43
Let Everyone Clap Hands Like Me

Traditional/Arranged by Mike Jackson

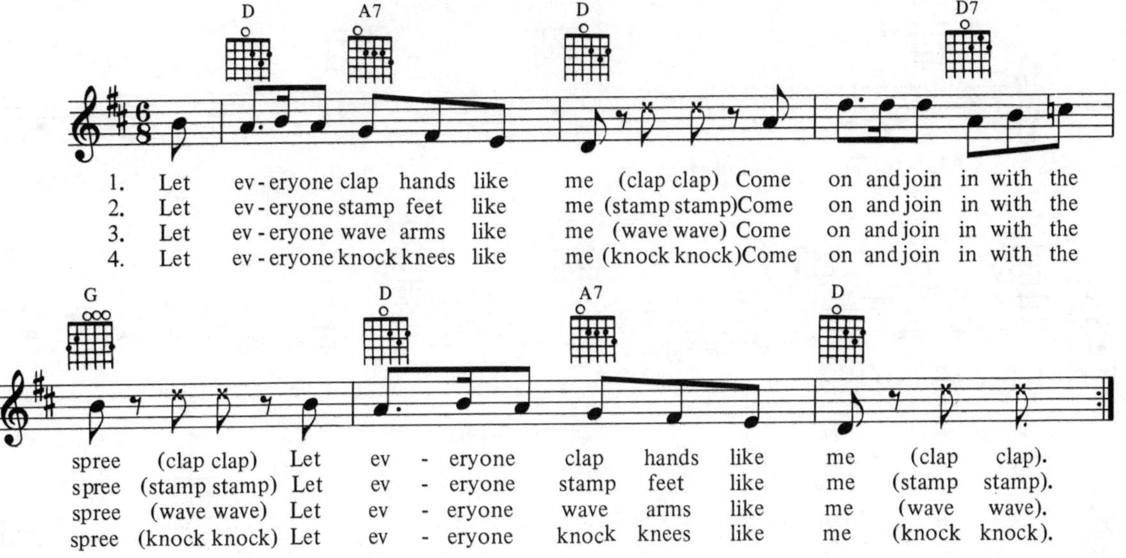
D
A7
D
D7
1. Let ev - eryone clap hands like me (clap clap) Come on and join in with the
2. Let ev - eryone stamp feet like me (stamp stamp) Come on and join in with the
3. Let ev - eryone wave arms like me (wave wave) Come on and join in with the
4. Let ev - eryone knock knees like me (knock knock) Come on and join in with the
G
D
A7
D
spree (clap clap) Let ev - eryone clap hands like me (clap clap).
spree (stamp stamp) Let ev - eryone stamp feet like me (stamp stamp).
spree (wave wave) Let ev - eryone wave arms like me (wave wave).
spree (knock knock) Let ev - eryone knock knees like me (knock knock).

44
The Little Skunk

Traditional/Arranged by Mike Jackson

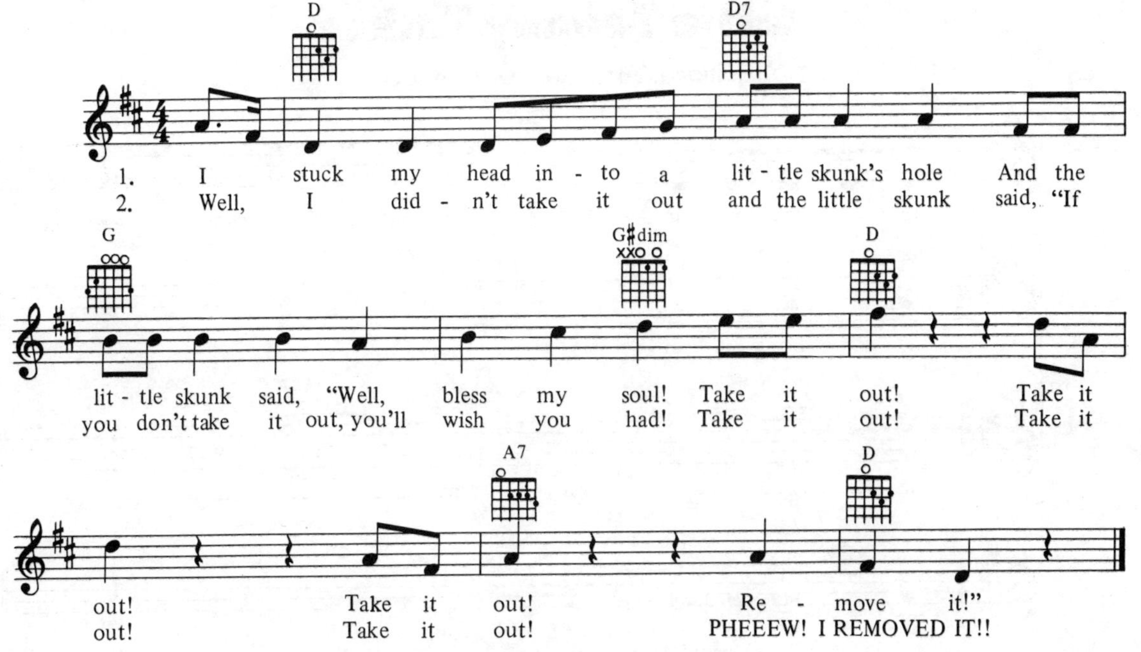
D
D7
1. I stuck my head in - to a lit - tle skunk's hole And the
2. Well, I did - n't take it out and the little skunk said, "If
G
G♯dim
D
lit - tle skunk said, "Well, bless my soul! Take it out! Take it
you don't take it out, you'll wish you had! Take it out! Take it
A7
D
out! Take it out! Re - move it!"
out! Take it out! PHEEEW! I REMOVED IT!!

45
Little Tommy Tadpole

Words: C. J. Dennis
Music: Mike & Michelle Jackson

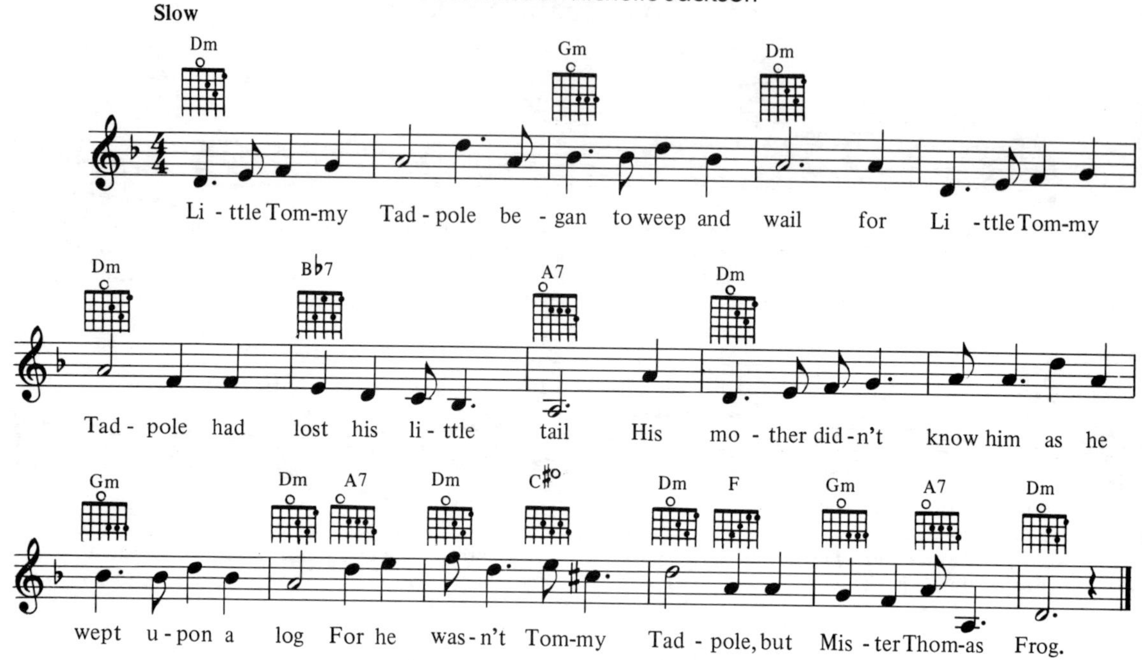
Slow
Dm
Gm
Dm
Li - ttle Tom-my Tad - pole be - gan to weep and wail for Li - ttle Tom-my
Dm
B♭7
A7
Dm
Tad - pole had lost his li - ttle tail His mo - ther did - n't know him as he
Gm
Dm
A7
Dm
C♯o
Dm
F
Gm
A7
Dm
wept u - pon a log For he was - n't Tom-my Tad - pole, but Mis - ter Thom - as Frog.

46
Little Tommy Tinker

Traditional/Arranged by Mike Jackson

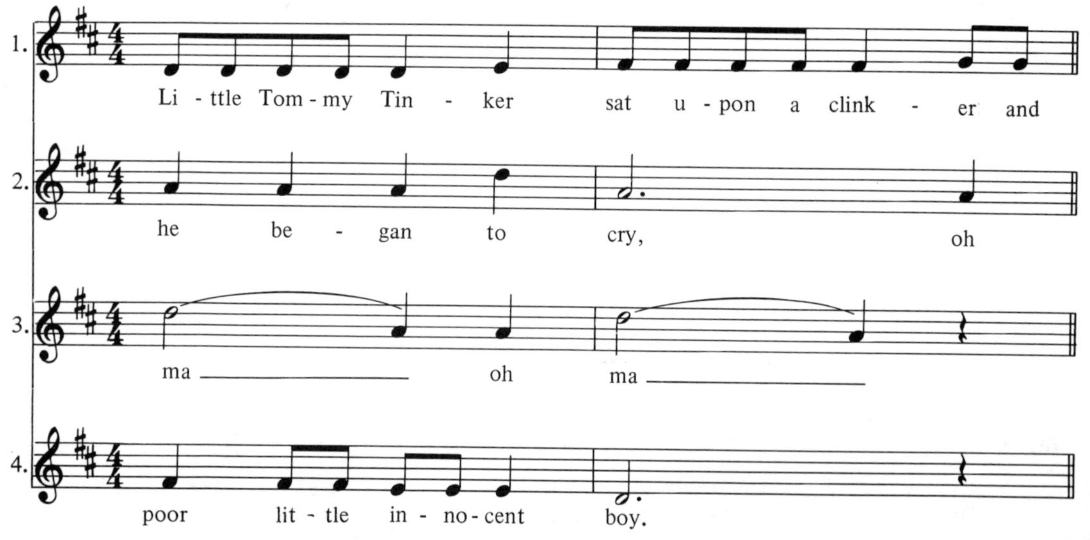
1.
Li - ttle Tom - my Tin - ker sat u - pon a clink - er and
2.
he be - gan to cry, oh
3.
ma oh ma
4.
poor lit - tle in - no - cent boy.

47
London Bridge

Traditional/Arranged by Mike Jackson

G
D
G
1. Lon - don Bridge is fall - ing down, fall - ing down, fall - ing down,
2. Build it up with sticks and stones, sticks and stones, sticks and stones,
3. Sticks and stones will all fall down, all fall down, all fall down,
4. Build it up with lumps of wood, lumps of wood, lumps of wood,
G
D
G
Lon - don Bridge is fall - ing down, my fair la - dy.
Build it up with sticks and stones, my fair la - dy.
Sticks and stones will all fall down, my fair la - dy.
Build it up with lumps of wood, my fair la - dy.

5. Lumps of wood will be no good, be no good, be no good,
   Lumps of wood will be no good, my fair lady.

6. Build it up with iron and steel, iron and steel, iron and steel,
   Build it up with iron and steel, my fair lady.

7. Iron and steel will bend and bow, bend and bow, bend and bow,
   Iron and steel will bend and bow, my fair lady.

8. Build it up with bricks so sure, bricks so sure, bricks so sure,
   Build it up with bricks so sure, my fair lady.

9. It will stand for evermore, evermore, evermore,
   It will stand for evermore, my fair lady.

48
Looby Loo

Traditional/Arranged by Mike Jackson

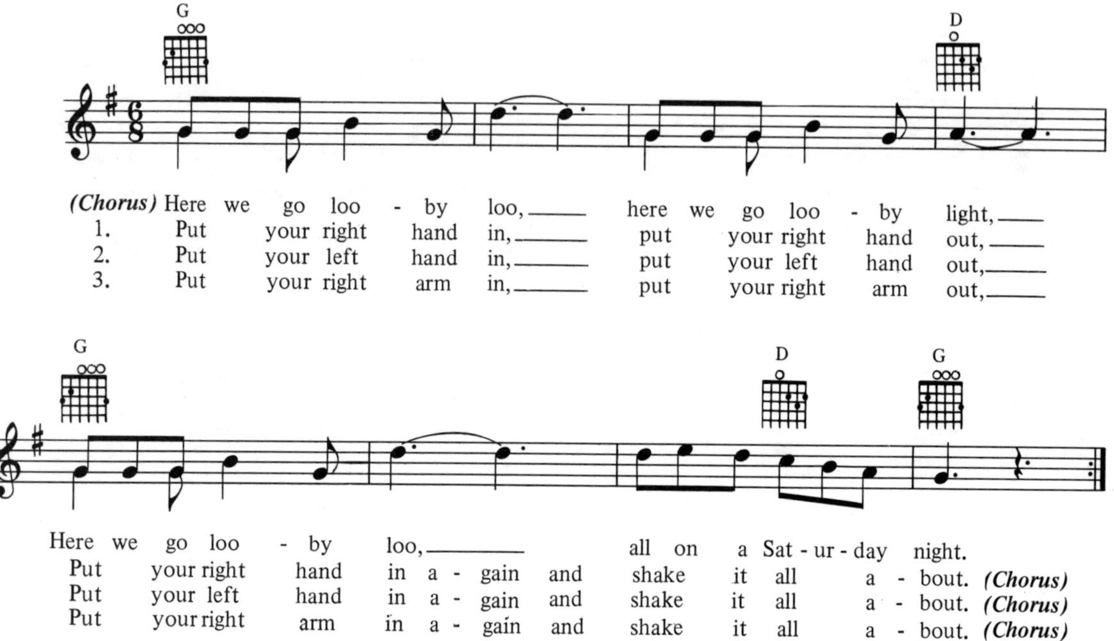

G
D
G
D
G
(Chorus) Here we go loo - by loo, here we go loo - by light,
1. Put your right hand in, put your right hand out,
2. Put your left hand in, put your left hand out,
3. Put your right arm in, put your right arm out,
Here we go loo - by loo, all on a Sat - ur - day night.
Put your right hand in a - gain and shake it all a - bout. (Chorus)
Put your left hand in a - gain and shake it all a - bout. (Chorus)
Put your right arm in a - gain and shake it all a - bout. (Chorus)

4. Put your left arm in,
 Put your left arm out
 Put your left arm in again
 And shake it all about.

(Chorus)

5. Put your right foot in,
 Put your right foot out,
 Put your right foot in again
 And shake it all about.

(Chorus)

6. Put your left foot in. . . .

(Chorus)

7. Right leg

(Chorus)

8. Left leg

(Chorus)

9. Back

(Chorus)

10. Front

(Chorus)

11. Head

(Chorus)

49

Love Makes The World Go Round

Words & Music by Mike & Michelle Jackson

Love makes the world go round: A smile is more val- ua - ble than all the gold that's under ground.
Last time to Coda
Love makes the world go round: Give a lit - tle love each day.
1. Grouch and your world goes flat
2. Sulk and your world goes grey Don't
Don't stamp your feet you might be stamp - ing on your hat! Grouch and your
stick your bottom lip out. It might trip you as you play! Sulk and your
would goes flat and it's not worth the trou - ble an - y way. Wear a
world goes grey and it's not worth the trou - ble an - y way. Don't
smile on your face as you're walk- ing down the street and you'll spread some hap - pi - ness to the
turn a-gainst your friends 'cos they've got a fault or two. Take a look in - to the mir - ror and
peop - le that you meet. Lend a help - ing hand to some - one in a mess and it
you'll see plen - ty too! For-giv - ing and for-getting is the way you keep your mates and it
makes the would a bet - ter place 'cos
makes the would a bet - ter place 'cos
D.C.
Coda
Give a lit - tle, get a lit - tle,
give a lit - tle, get a lit - tle, Give a lit - tle love each day.

50
The Marvellous Toy

Words & Music by Tom Paxton

A7 D A7 D
1. When I was just a wee lit - tle lad, full of health and
2. The first time that I picked it up I had a big sur -
3. It first marched left and then marched right and then marched under a
4. Well, the years have gone by too quickly, it seems, I have my own little
A7 G D E7 A7
joy, My fath - er home - ward came one night and gave to me a toy. A
prise For right on its bottom were two big buttons that looked like big green eyes. I
chair And when I looked where it had gone, it was - n't ev - en there! I
boy And yes - ter - day I gave to him my marvell - ous lit - tle toy. His
D A7 D G
won - der to be hold it was, with man - y col - ours bright. And the
first pushed one and then the other, and then I twisted its lid And
started to sob and my dad - dy laughed, for he knew that I would find, When I
eyes nearly popped right out of his head and he gave a squeal of glee, Neither
G D A7 D A7
mo - ment I laid eyes on it, It be - came my heart's de - light. It went
when I set it down a - gain, this is what it did: It went
turned a - round, my marvell - ous toy, chug - ging from be - hind. It went
one of us knows just what it is, but he loves it, just like me. It went
Chorus
D A7 D G
'zip' when it moved, and — 'bop' when it stopped and 'whirr' when it stood still. I
G D A7 D
nev - er knew just what it was, And I guess I nev - er will.

Last Chorus:

It still goes Zip when it moves and Bop when it stops
And Whir-r-r when it stands still.
I never knew just what it was
And I guess I never will.

51
Me And My Teddy Bear

Words & Music by Fred Coots & Jack Winters

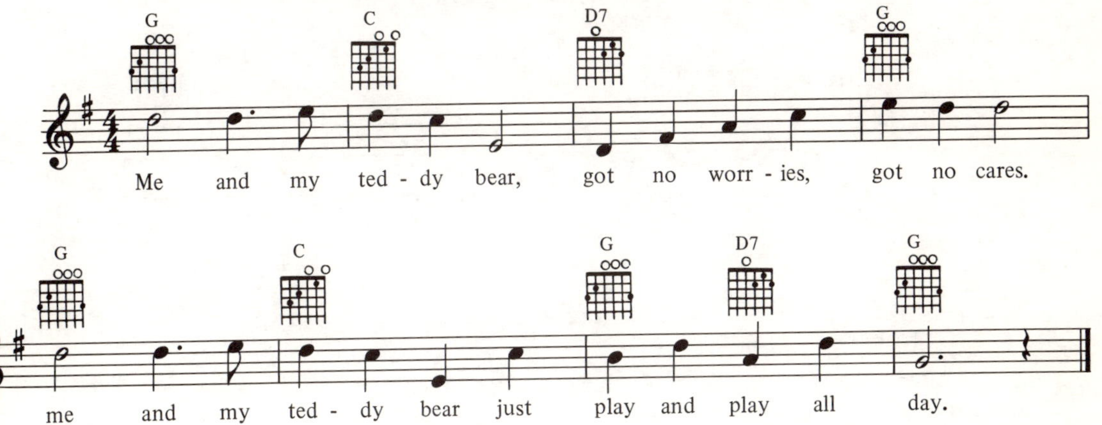
G
C
D7
G
Me and my ted - dy bear, got no worr - ies, got no cares.
G
C
G
D7
G
me and my ted - dy bear just play and play all day.

52
Miss Polly Had A Dolly

Traditional/Arranged by Mike & Michelle Jackson

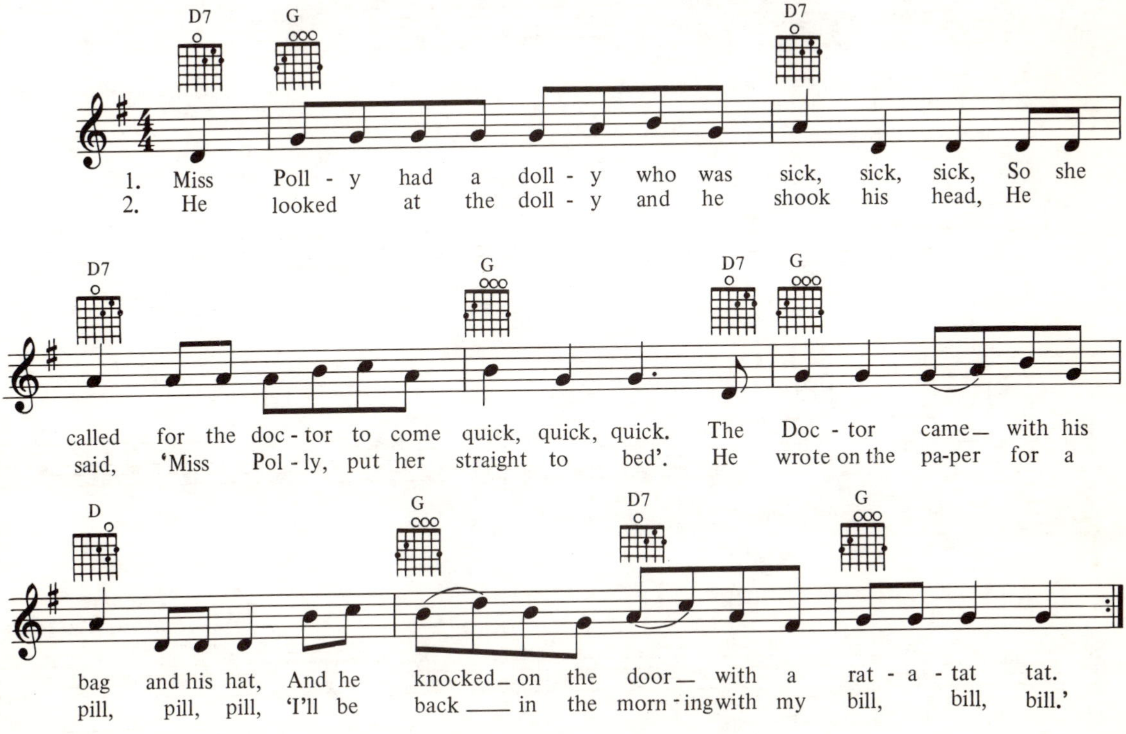

D7 G D7

1. Miss Poll - y had a doll - y who was sick, sick, sick, So she
2. He looked at the doll - y and he shook his head, He

D7 G D7 G

called for the doc - tor to come quick, quick, quick. The Doc - tor came — with his
said, 'Miss Pol - ly, put her straight to bed'. He wrote on the pa-per for a

D G D7 G

bag and his hat, And he knocked — on the door — with a rat - a - tat tat.
pill, pill, pill, 'I'll be back — in the morn - ing with my bill, bill, bill.'

53
Nellie The Elephant

Words: Ralph Butler
Music: Peter Hart

Dm A7 Dm A7
1. To Bom - bay, a tra - ve - lling cir - cus came. They
2. Night by night, she danced to the cir - cus band. While
E7 A E7 A7
brought an in - tell - i - gent El - e - phant and Ne - lly was her name.
Ne - lly was lea - ding the big pa - rade. She looked so proud and grand.
Dm A7 Dm A7 E7 A
One dark night. she slipped her i - ron chain and off she went to Hin - du - stan and was
No more tricks. for Ne - lly to per - form. They taught her how to take a bow And she
E7 A7 D
Chorus
ne - ver seen a - gain. Oh Ne - lly the El - e - phant packed her trunk and
took the crowd by storm. So.
G D A7 D
said good - bye to the cir - cus. Off she went with a trump - e - ty trump.
A E7 A7 D
Trump. Trump. Trump Ne - lly the El - e - phant packed her trunk and
G D A7 D
2nd time through go to
trun - dled back to the jung - le Off she went with a trump - e - ty trump.

Em A7 D D7 G A7 D

Trump, Trump, Trump. The head of the herd was call - ing From far far a-way, They

E7 A E7 A A7

met one night in the sil - very light On the road to Man - da - lay, So

D G D

Ne - lly the El - e - phant packed her trunk and said good-bye to the cir - cus.

A7 D G A7 D

Off she went with a trump - e - ty trump. Trump, Trump, Trump.

G A G A G A7 D

Trump, Trump, Trump, Trump, Trump, Trump, Trump, ump_ump ump.

54
My Hat It Has Three Corners

Traditional/Arranged by Mike Jackson

D A7 D
My hat it has three cor-ners,_ three cor-ners has my hat. If it
D A7 D
did-n't_ have three cor-ners,_ then it would-n't_ be my hat.

55
Nicky Knacky Knocky Noo

Traditional/Arranged by Mike Jackson

G
1. With my hands on my head, what have I
2. With my hands on my eyes, what have I
3. With my hands on my nose, what have I
D
G
here? This is my main think - er my teach - er
here? These are my eye peep - ers my teach - er
here? This is my smell box - er my teach - er
1.
G
D7
dear Main think - er Nick - y knach- y knack-y noo. That's what they
D7
G
2.-9.
G
Repeats
taught me when I went to school. Main think - er 2) eye - peep - ers
3) smell box - er
Nick - y knack-y knock-y noo. That's what they taught me when I went to school.

4. With my hands on my mouth,
   What have I here?
   This is my chatterboxer,
   My teacher dear.
   Main thinker, eye peepers, smell
   boxer, chatterboxer,
   Nicky, knacky, knocky, noo.
   That's what they taught me
   When I went to school.

5. This is my chin wagger
6. This is my cough chester
7. This is my bread basket
8. These are my knee knockers
9. These are my toe tappers

56
Ob-la-di, Ob-la-da

Words & Music by John Lennon & Paul McCartney

E
B7
1. Des-mond has a bar-row in the mar - ket place, Mol - ly is the
2. Des-mond takes a trol - ley to the jeweller's store, Buys a twen- ty
3. Hap - py ev - er aft - er in the mar - ket place Des - mond lets the
E
sing - er in a band. Des - mond says to Mol - ly, "Girl, I
car - at gold - en ring. Takes it back to Mol - ly, wait - ing
child - ren lend a hand. Mol - ly stays at home and does her
A
E
B7
E
like your face," And Mol - ly says this as she takes him by the hand,
at the door And as he gives it to her she be - gins to sing. . .
pret - ty face And in the even - ing she still sings it with the band.
E
G♯m
C♯m
E
B7
E
Ob-la - di ob-la - da, Life goes on, Bra la - la, how the life goes on.
To Coda
G♯m
C♯m
E
B7
E
Ob- la - di ob-la - da Life goes on, Bra la - la, how the life goes on.
1.2.
3.
E7
A
E
F♯m
E
E7
In a couple of years they have built a home sweet home
A
E
B7
D.S. al Coda
With a couple of kids run-ning in the yard of Des-mond and Mol - ly Jones.
Coda
C♯m
B7
E
And if you want some fun Sing Ob-la - di-bla da.

57
Old Hogan's Goat

Traditional/Arranged by Mike Jackson

G7 C C7 F
1. There was a man Now please take note
(2nd voice) There was a man Now please take
2. One day that goat Was feel - ing fine
One day that goat Was feel - ing
3. Now when the train Came in - to sight
Now when the train Came in - to

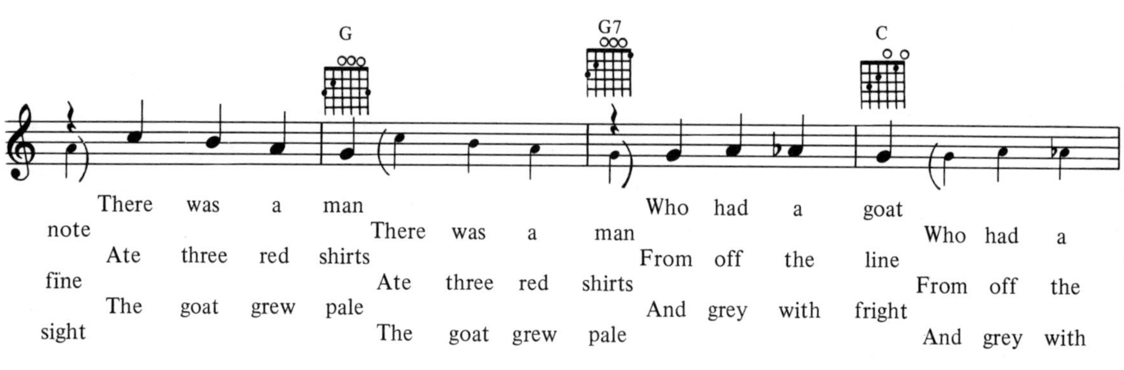
G G7 C
There was a man Who had a goat
note There was a man Who had a
Ate three red shirts From off the line
fine Ate three red shirts From off the
The goat grew pale And grey with fright
sight The goat grew pale And grey with

G7 C C7 F

He loved that goat In - deed he did
goat He loved that goat In - deed he
The old man grabbed Her by the back
line The old man grabbed Her by the
She struggl - ed hard And then a - gain
fright She struggl - ed hard And then a -

G7 C

He loved that goat Just like a kid.
did He loved that goat Just like a kid.
And tied her to The rail - way track.
back And tied her to The rail - way track.
Coughed up the shirts And flagged the train.
gain Coughed up the shirts And flagged the train.

58
Once In Royal David's City

Mrs C.F. Alexander/Arranged by Mike Jackson

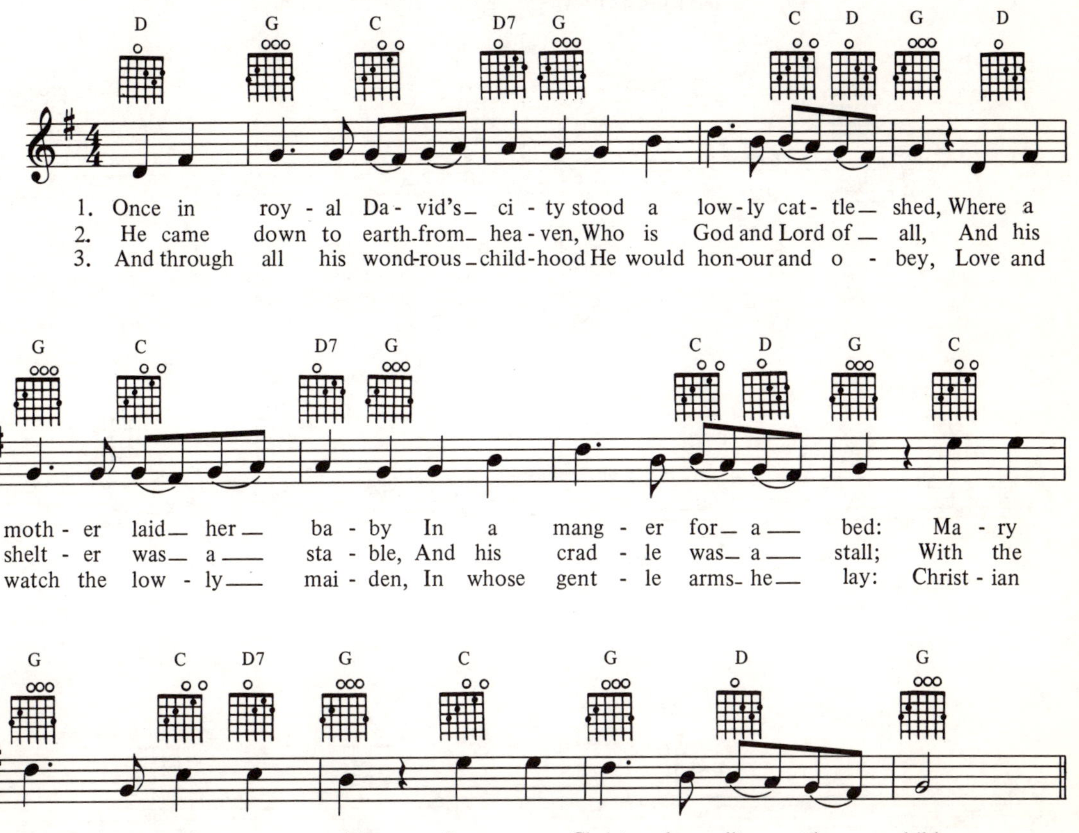
D G C D7 G C D G D
1. Once in roy - al Da - vid's ci - ty stood a low - ly cat - tle shed, Where a
2. He came down to earth from hea - ven, Who is God and Lord of all, And his
3. And through all his wond-rous child-hood He would hon-our and o - bey, Love and
G C D7 G C D G C
moth - er laid her ba - by In a mang - er for a bed: Ma - ry
shelt - er was a sta - ble, And his crad - le was a stall; With the
watch the low - ly mai - den, In whose gent - le arms he lay: Christ - ian
G C D7 G C G D G
was that moth - er mild Jes - us Christ her lit - tle child.
poor, and mean, and lowly, Lived on earth our Sav - iour holy.
child - ren all must be Mild, ob - ed - ient go-od as he.

4. For he is our childhood's pattern:
   Day by day like us he grew,
   He was little, weak, and helpless,
   Tears and smiles like us he knew;
   And he feeleth for our sadness,
   And he shareth in our gladness.

5. And our eyes at last shall see him,
   Through his own redeeming love,
   For that child so dear and gentle
   Is our Lord in heaven above;
   And he leads his children on
   To the place where he is gone.

59
One Elephant Went Out To Play

Traditional/Arranged by Mike Jackson

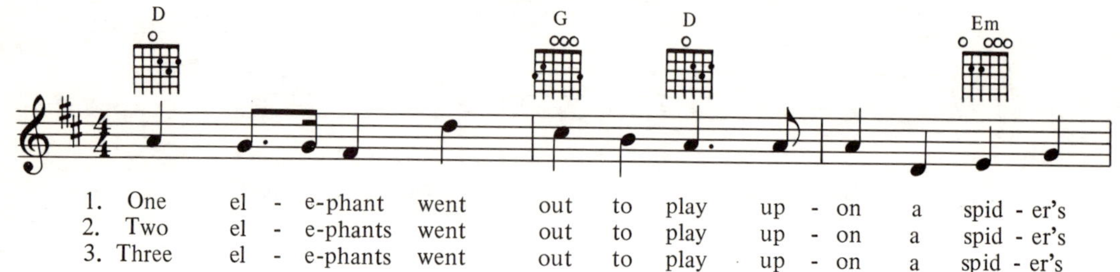
D
G
D
Em
1. One el - e-phant went out to play up - on a spid - er's
2. Two el - e-phants went out to play up - on a spid - er's
3. Three el - e-phants went out to play up - on a spid - er's

A
D
G
D
web one day, he was hav - ing such e - norm - ous fun That he
web one day, they were hav - ing such e - norm - ous fun That they
web one day, they were hav - ing such e - norm - ous fun That they

G
A
D
called for a - noth - er el - e - phant to come.
called for a - noth - er el - e - phant to come.
called for a - noth - er el - e - phant to come.

and so on through "Four elephants", "Five elephants" etc. The final verse ends with:

They were having such enormous fun
But there were no more elephants left to come.

60
One Finger One Thumb

Traditional/Arranged by Mike Jackson

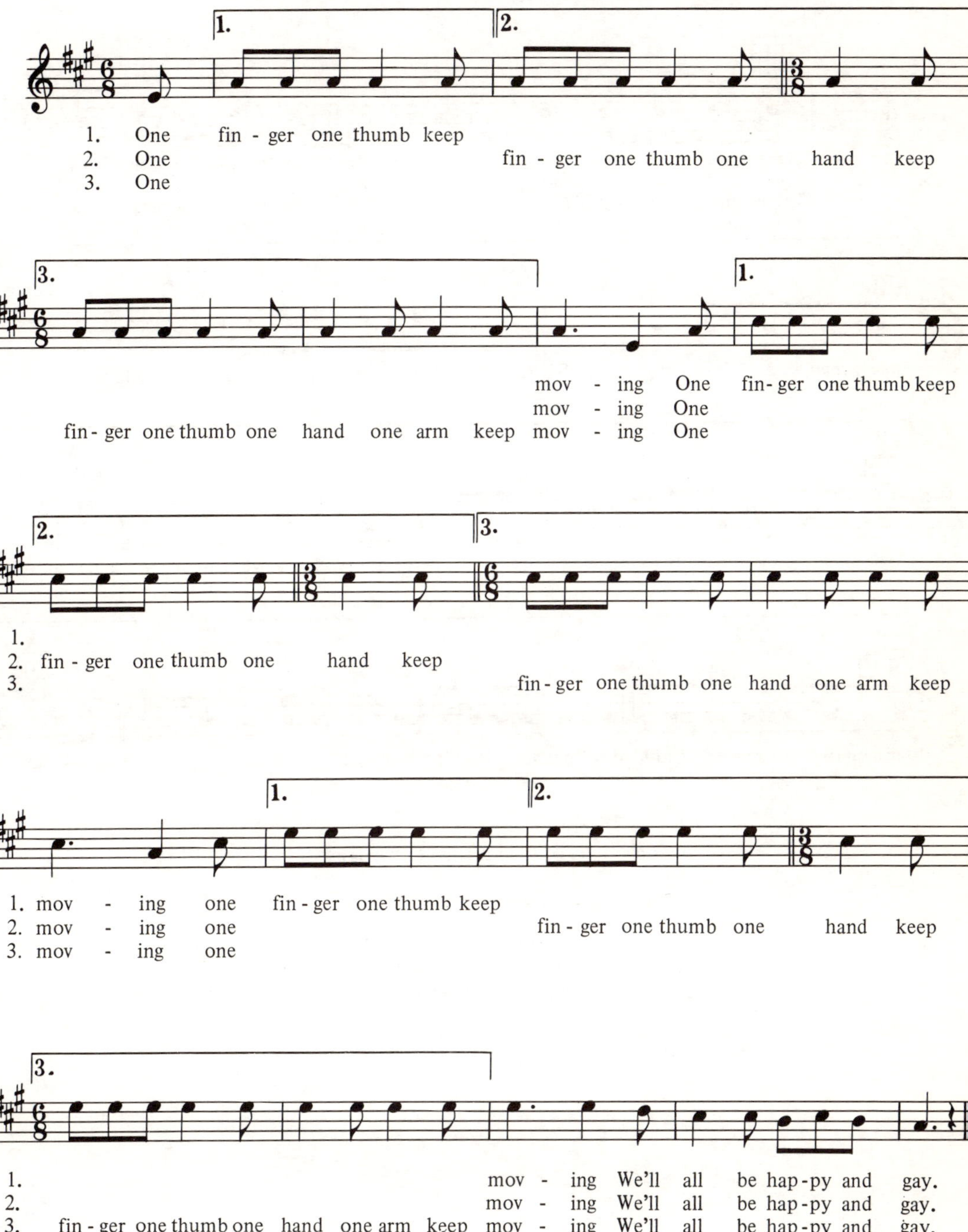
1.
2.
1. One fin - ger one thumb keep
2. One fin - ger one thumb one hand keep
3. One
3.
1.
mov - ing One fin- ger one thumb keep
mov - ing One
fin - ger one thumb one hand one arm keep mov - ing One
2.
3.
1.
2. fin - ger one thumb one hand keep
3. fin - ger one thumb one hand one arm keep
1.
2.
1. mov - ing one fin - ger one thumb keep
2. mov - ing one fin - ger one thumb one hand keep
3. mov - ing one
3.
1. mov - ing We'll all be hap - py and gay.
2. mov - ing We'll all be hap - py and gay.
3. fin - ger one thumb one hand one arm keep mov - ing We'll all be hap - py and gay.

. . . and so on through head, toe, foot, leg, etc.

61
One Man Went To Mow

Traditional/Arranged by Mike Jackson

G
D7
1. One man & his dog, went to mow a mea - dow
2. Two men ment to mow, went to mow a mea - dow
3. Three men ment to mow, went to mow a mea - dow
4. Four men ment to mow, went to mow a mea - dow
1. D7
G
one man & his dog, Spot, want to mow a mea - dow
2. D7
G
Two men one man & his dog, Spot & a saus - age roll, went to mow a mea-dow
3. D7
G
three men two men one man and his dog, Spot, and a saus-age roll, and a pint of milk, went to mow a mea-dow

4. Four men. . . . . .and a can of beans etc.

5. Five men. . . . . . . .and a magazine.

6. Six men went to mow but they didn't mow the meadow.
They were too busy reading magazines, eating beans, drinking milk and feeding the dog with the sausage roll to get out and mow the meadow!

62
One Two Three Four Five

Traditional/Arranged by Mike Jackson

G D7
One two three four five, once I caught a fish a - live

D7 D A7 D7
Six sev - en eight nine ten, then I let him go a - gain

G D7
Why did you let him go? Be - cause he bit my fin - ger so,

D7 G
Which fin - ger did he bite, this lit - tle fing - er on the right

63
On Top Of Spaghetti

Traditional/Arranged by Mike Jackson

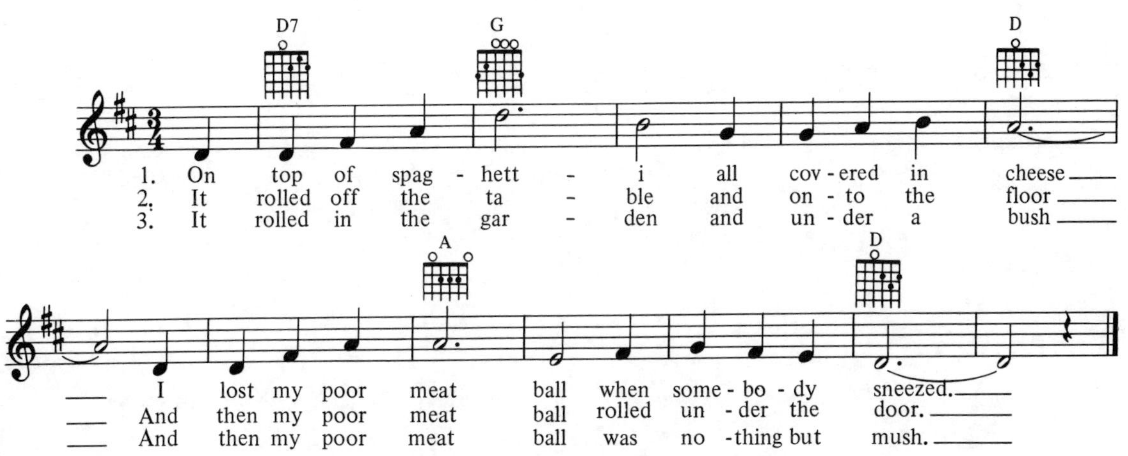
D7 G D
1. On top of spag - hett - i all cov - ered in cheese
2. It rolled off the ta - ble and on - to the floor
3. It rolled in the gar - den and un - der a bush
A D
I lost my poor meat ball when some - bo - dy sneezed.
And then my poor meat ball rolled un - der the door.
And then my poor meat ball was no - thing but mush.

64
Oranges And Lemons

Traditional/Arranged by Mike Jackson

G
D7
G
Orang - es and lem - ons say the bells of St Clem - ents, you
Owe me five far - things say the bells of St Martins
D
A7
D
When will you pay me say the bells of Old Bail - ey When I grow
A7
D7
G
rich say the bells of Shore - ditch When will that be say the
D7
G
D
A7
D7
bells of Step - ney I do not know says the great bell of Bow.
G
D7
G
Here comes the can - dle to light you to bed, And here comes the
D7
G
chop - per to chop off your head. Chop! Chop! Chop!

65
The Owl And The Pussy-cat

Poem by Edward Lear (P.D.)
Music: Traditional/Arranged by Mike Jackson

G D G D
1. The Owl and the Pussy - Cat went to sea in a beaut - i - ful pea - green
2. Pussy said to the Owl, "you ele - gant fowl, how charm - ing-ly sweet you
3. Dear pig, are you will - ing to sell for one shill-ing Your ring?" Said the Piggy,
G D
boat; They took some hon - ey and plen - ty of mon - ey wrapped
sing! Oh let us be mar - ried; too long we have tar - ried, But
"I will." So they took it a - way and were mar - ried next day By the
G D G C G C G
up in a five pound note. The Owl looked up to the stars a - bove, And
what shall we do for a ring?" They sailed a - way for a year and a day To the
tur - key who lives on the hill. They dined on mince and slices of quince, Which they
Em A7 D
a tempo
sang to a small guit - ar, "O love - ly pus - sy, O
land where the bong - tree grows; And there in the woods a
ate with a run - cible spoon; And hand in hand, on the
C Am D G
Pus - sy, my love, what a beaut - i - ful Pus - sy you are, you
piggy - wig stood with a ring on the end of his nose, his
edge of the sand, They danced by the light of the moon, the
Em G D7 G
are, you are, What a beau - ti - ful Pus - sy you are.
nose, his nose. With a ring on the end of his nose.
moon, the moon, They danced by the light of the moon.

66
Peanut Butter Sandwich

Traditional/Arranged by Mike Jackson
Words Adapted by Mike Jackson

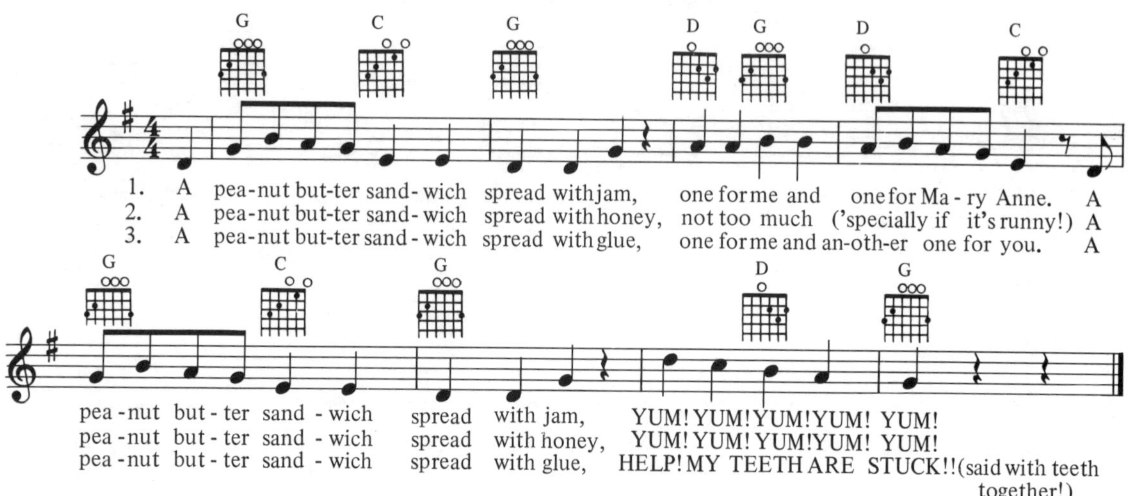
G C G D G D C
1. A pea-nut but-ter sand-wich spread with jam, one for me and one for Ma-ry Anne. A
2. A pea-nut but-ter sand-wich spread with honey, not too much ('specially if it's runny!) A
3. A pea-nut but-ter sand-wich spread with glue, one for me and an-oth-er one for you. A
G C G D G
pea-nut but-ter sand-wich spread with jam, YUM! YUM! YUM! YUM! YUM!
pea-nut but-ter sand-wich spread with honey, YUM! YUM! YUM! YUM! YUM!
pea-nut but-ter sand-wich spread with glue, HELP! MY TEETH ARE STUCK!! (said with teeth together!)

67
Polly Wolly Doodle

Words: Traditional/Adapted by Mike Jackson
Music: Traditional/Arranged by Mike Jackson

G D
Oh my Sal she is a — mai-den fair Sing-ing Poll-y Woll-y Doo-dle all the day. With —
Grass-hopper sittin' on a rail-road track Sing-ing Poll-y Woll-y Doo-dle all the day.
Grass-hopper still on the rail-road track Sing-ing Poll-y Woll-y Doo-dle all the day.

D D7 G
lau-ghing eyes and — cur-ly hair. Singing — Pol-ly Wol-ly Doo-dle all the day. Fare thee
Train came roar-ing — over his back. Singing — Pol-ly Wol-ly Doo-dle all the day.
Twenty miles forward and — ten miles back. Singing — Pol-ly Wol-ly Doo-dle all the day.

G D7
well Fare thee well Fare thee well my fairly — fay for I'm off to Louis-i-an-a for to

D7 G
see my Su-zy-An-na Sing-ing Pol-ly Wol-ly Doo-dle all the Day!

68
Pretty Little Dutch Girl

Traditional/Arranged by Mike Jackson

D
G
D
1. I am a pret - ty lit - tle Dutch girl As
2. I hate to do the dish - es I
3. My boy - friend's name is To - ny He
4. One day when I was walk - ing I
5. I L - O - V - E love you I
G
A
D
G
pret - ty as pret - ty can be be be And all the boys in the
hate to scrub the floor I love to kiss my
lives on ma - ca - ro - ni With a freckle on his nose and
saw my boy - friend talk - ing To a pretty little girl with
K - I - S - S kiss you so I jumped in the lake and
A
G
A
D
base - ball team Go cra - zy o - ver me me me.
boy - friend Be - hind the kit - chen door.
forty - eight toes And this is how my sto - ry goes.
strawber - ry curls And this is what he said to her.
swallowed a snake And came up with a bel - ly ache.

69
Punchinello

Traditional/Arranged by Mike Jackson & Alan Craig

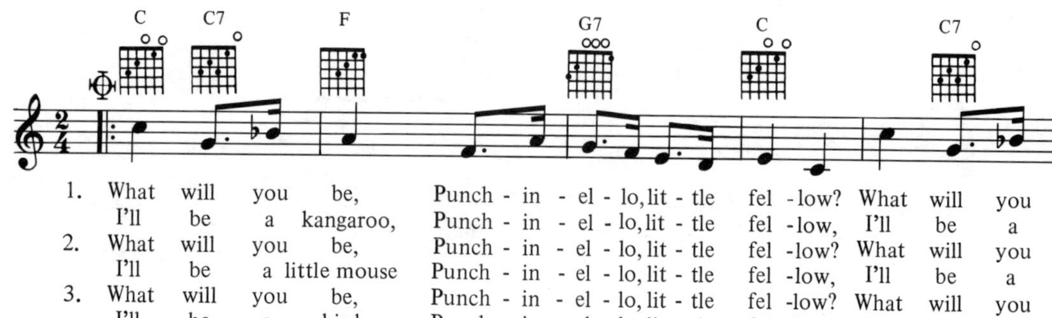
C
C7
F
G7
C
C7
1. What will you be, Punch - in - el - lo, lit - tle fel - low? What will you
I'll be a kangaroo, Punch - in - el - lo, lit - tle fel - low, I'll be a
2. What will you be, Punch - in - el - lo, lit - tle fel - low? What will you
I'll be a little mouse Punch - in - el - lo, lit - tle fel - low, I'll be a
3. What will you be, Punch - in - el - lo, lit - tle fel - low? What will you
I'll be a bird, Punch - in - el - lo, lit - tle fel - low, I'll be a

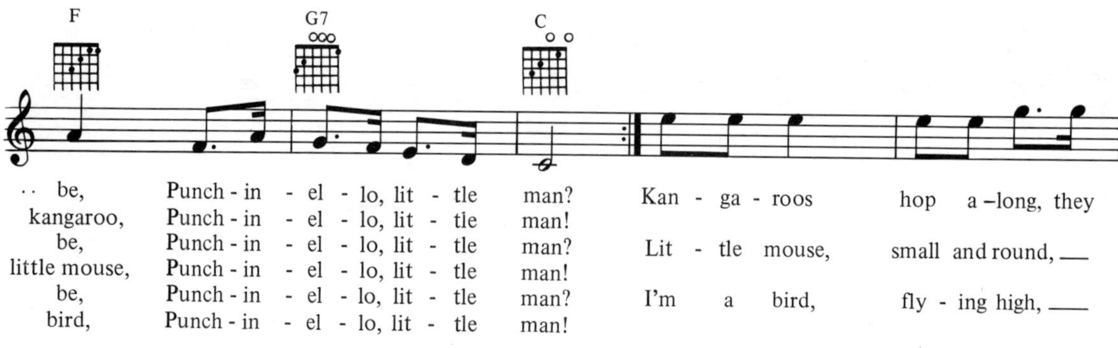
F
G7
C
be, Punch - in - el - lo, lit - tle man? Kan - ga - roos hop a – long, they
kangaroo, Punch - in - el - lo, lit - tle man!
be, Punch - in - el - lo, lit - tle man? Lit - tle mouse, small and round,
little mouse, Punch - in - el - lo, lit - tle man!
be, Punch - in - el - lo, lit - tle man? I'm a bird, fly - ing high,
bird, Punch - in - el - lo, lit - tle man!

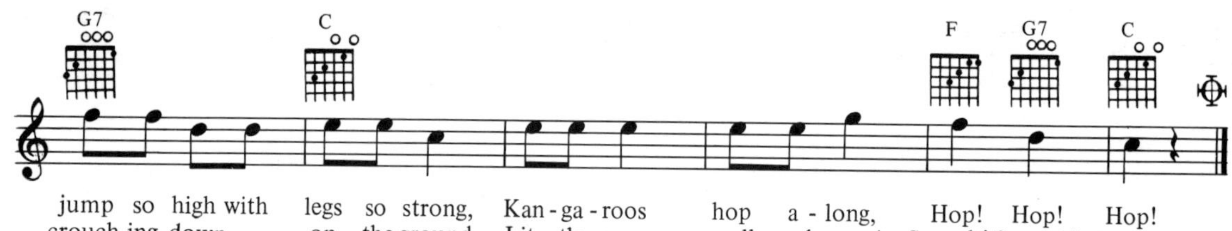
G7
C
F
G7
C
jump so high with legs so strong, Kan - ga - roos hop a - long, Hop! Hop! Hop!
crouch-ing down, on the ground, Lit - tle mouse, small and round, Squeak! Squeak! Squeak!
way up high, in the sky, I'm a bird, fly - ing high, Flap! Flap! Flap!

4. What will you be, Punchinello, little fellow?
What will you be, Punchinello, little man?

I'll be a horse, Punchinello, little fellow,
I'll be a horse, Punchinello, little man!

I'm a horse, trotting fast,
Across the fields, through the grass,
I'm a horse trotting fast,
Trot! Trot! Trot!

5. What will you be, ... ?

I'll be an elephant, . . . !

Swing my trunk side to side,
Swing it low and swing it wide,
Swing my trunk side to side,
Stomp! Stomp! Stomp!

6. What will you be, ... ?

I'll be a crocodile, ... !

I'm a crocodile so scary,
My big jaws make people wary,
I'm a crocodile so scary,
Snap! Snap! Snap!

70
The Quartermaster's Store

Traditional/Arranged by Mike Jackson

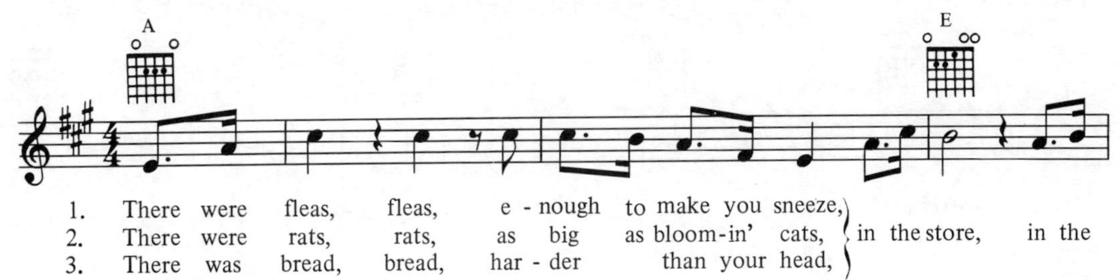
A
E
1. There were fleas, fleas, e - nough to make you sneeze,
2. There were rats, rats, as big as bloom-in' cats,
3. There was bread, bread, har - der than your head,
in the store, in the

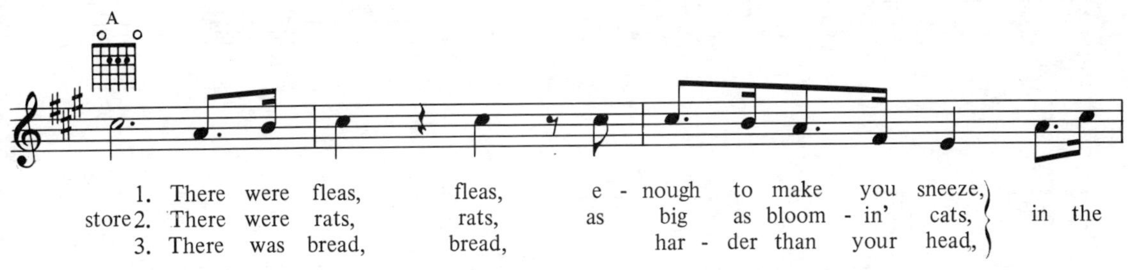
A
store
1. There were fleas, fleas, e - nough to make you sneeze,
2. There were rats, rats, as big as bloom - in' cats,
3. There was bread, bread, har - der than your head,
in the

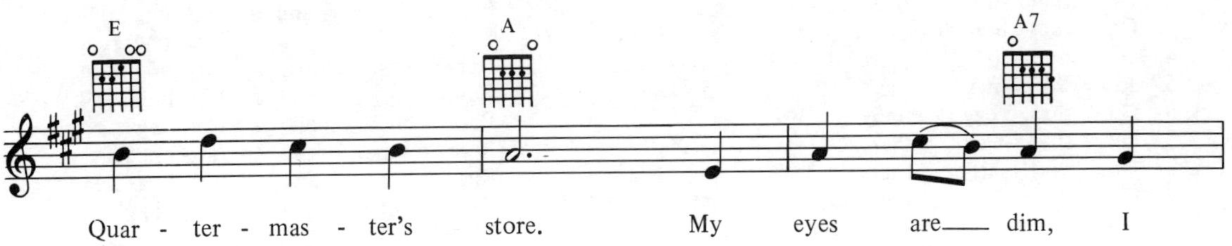
E
A
A7
Quar - ter - mas - ter's store. My eyes are dim, I

D
E7
can - not see, I have not brought my specs with me, I

A
D
E7
A
have not brought my specs with me.

71
Rattling Bog

Traditional/Arranged by Mike Jackson

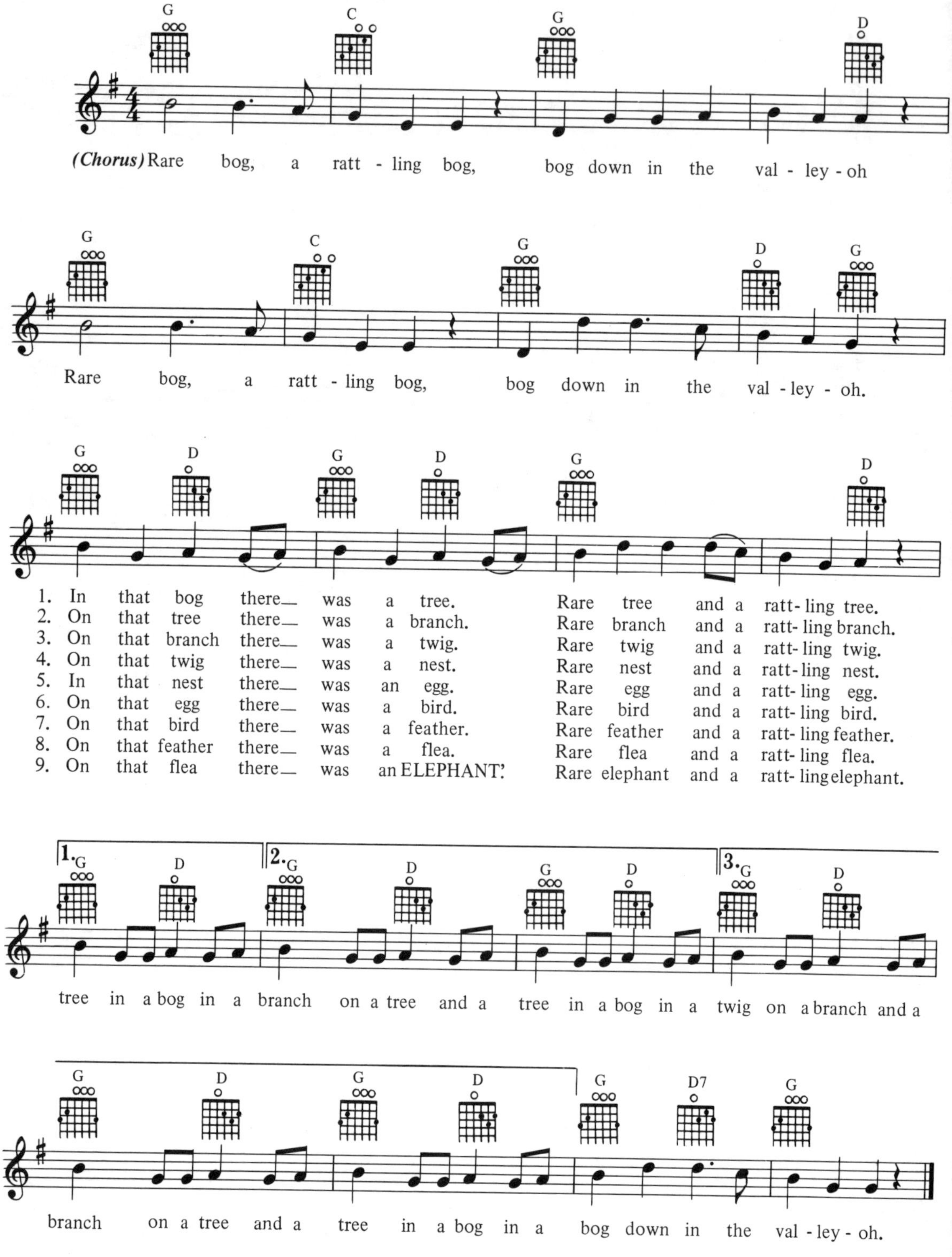

G C G D

(Chorus) Rare bog, a ratt - ling bog, bog down in the val - ley - oh

G C G D G

Rare bog, a ratt - ling bog, bog down in the val - ley - oh.

G D G D G D

1. In that bog there— was a tree. Rare tree and a ratt- ling tree.
2. On that tree there— was a branch. Rare branch and a ratt- ling branch.
3. On that branch there— was a twig. Rare twig and a ratt- ling twig.
4. On that twig there— was a nest. Rare nest and a ratt- ling nest.
5. In that nest there— was an egg. Rare egg and a ratt- ling egg.
6. On that egg there— was a bird. Rare bird and a ratt- ling bird.
7. On that bird there— was a feather. Rare feather and a ratt- ling feather.
8. On that feather there— was a flea. Rare flea and a ratt- ling flea.
9. On that flea there— was an ELEPHANT! Rare elephant and a ratt- ling elephant.

1. G D 2. G D G D 3. G D

tree in a bog in a branch on a tree and a tree in a bog in a twig on a branch and a

G D G D G D7 G
branch on a tree and a tree in a bog in a bog down in the val - ley - oh.

72
Rig-A-Jig-Jig

Traditional/Arranged by
Mike & Michelle Jackson & Alan Craig

D
Bm
A7
Bm
1. Rig - a - jig - jig and a - way we go, a - way we go, a - way we go,
2. In - to the mid - dle and back a - gain, back a - gain, back a - gain,
3. Turn to your part - ner and clap their hands, , clap their hands, clap their hands,
4. Hold their hands and swing them round, swing them round, swing them round,

D
Bm
A7
D
Rig - a - jig - jig and a - way we go, all a - round the cir - cle.
In - to the mid - dle and back a - gain, all a - round the cir - cle.
Turn to your part - ner and clap their hands, all a - round the cir - cle.
Hold their hands and swing them round, all a - round the cir - cle.

73
Ring-A-Ring-A-Rosie

Traditional/Arranged by Mike Jackson

G
C
D
G
Ring - a - ring - a - ro - sie. A pocket full of po - sies. A - tish - oo! A-tish oo! We all fall down

74
Rock-A-Bye Baby

Traditional/Arranged by Mike Jackson

D A D

1. Rock - a - bye ba - by on the tree top.
2. Rock - a - bye ba - by, no - thing to fear,

D A7 D

When the wind blows, the cra - dle will rock.
While you are sleep - ing Mum - my is near.

D G Em

When the bow breaks, the cra - dle will fall,
Sleep in your crad - le so safe and sound.

D G A7 D

Down will come ba - by cra - dle and all.
No - thing can harm you while Mum - my's a - round.

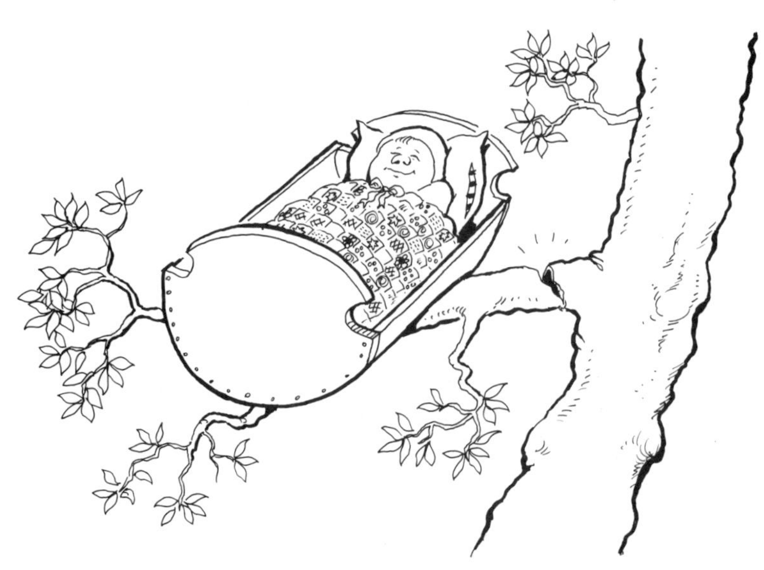

75
Row, Row, Row Your Boat

Words: Traditional
Music: Traditional/Arranged by
Mike & Michelle Jackson

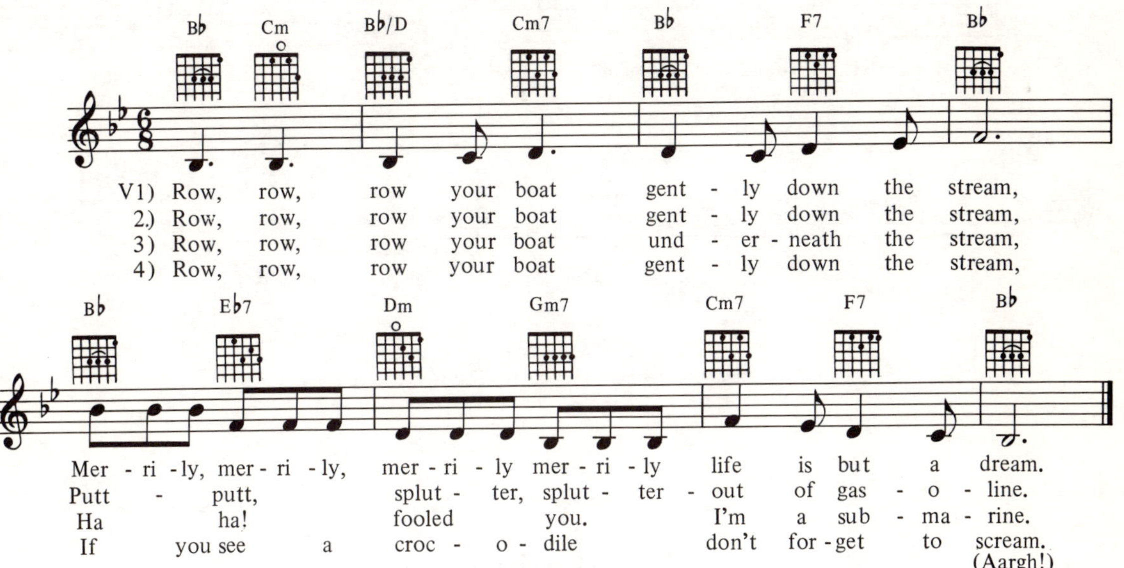

B♭ Cm B♭/D Cm7 B♭ F7 B♭
V1) Row, row, row your boat gent - ly down the stream,
2.) Row, row, row your boat gent - ly down the stream,
3) Row, row, row your boat und - er - neath the stream,
4) Row, row, row your boat gent - ly down the stream,
B♭ E♭7 Dm Gm7 Cm7 F7 B♭
Mer - ri - ly, mer - ri - ly, mer - ri - ly mer - ri - ly life is but a dream.
Putt - putt, splut - ter, splut - ter - out of gas - o - line.
Ha ha! fooled you. I'm a sub - ma - rine.
If you see a croc - o - dile don't for - get to scream.
(Aargh!)

GAS

76
Sally Go Round The Sun

Traditional/Arranged by Mike Jackson

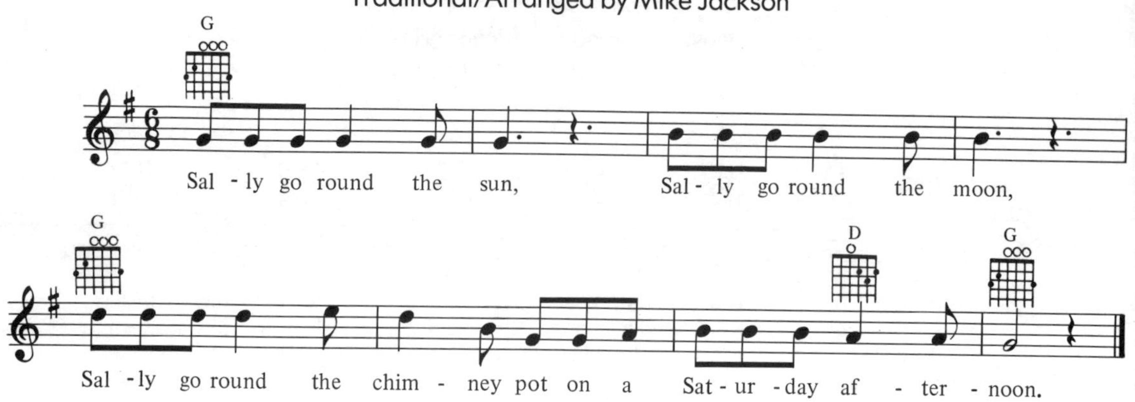
G
Sal - ly go round the sun, Sal - ly go round the moon,
G
D
G
Sal - ly go round the chim - ney pot on a Sat - ur - day af - ter - noon.

77
Sandwiches

Words & Music by Bob King

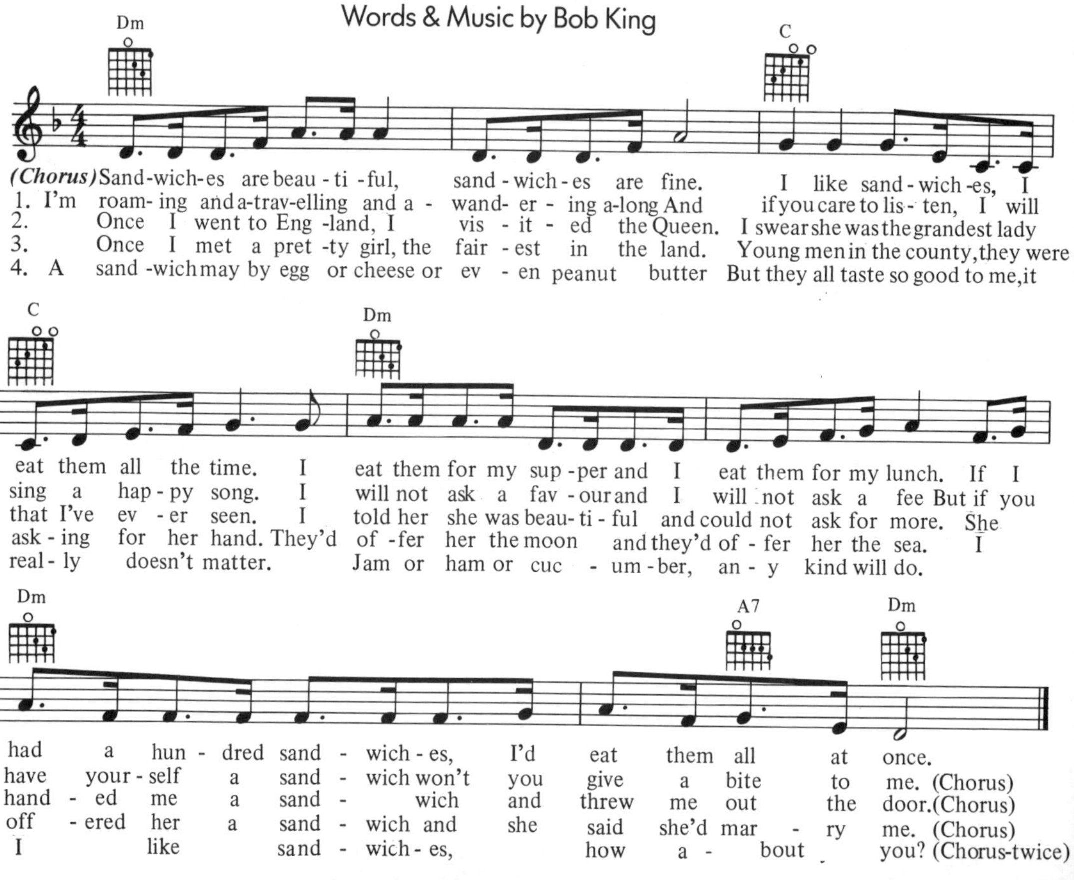

Dm C C Dm Dm A7 Dm

(Chorus) Sand-wich-es are beau - ti - ful, sand - wich - es are fine. I like sand - wich - es, I eat them all the time. I eat them for my sup - per and I eat them for my lunch. If I had a hun - dred sand - wich - es, I'd eat them all at once.

1. I'm roam - ing and a-trav-elling and a - wand - er - ing a-long And if you care to lis - ten, I will sing a hap - py song. I will not ask a fav - our and I will not ask a fee But if you have your - self a sand - wich won't you give a bite to me. (Chorus)
2. Once I went to Eng - land, I vis - it - ed the Queen. I swear she was the grandest lady that I've ev - er seen. I told her she was beau - ti - ful and could not ask for more. She hand - ed me a sand - wich and threw me out the door. (Chorus)
3. Once I met a pret - ty girl, the fair - est in the land. Young men in the county, they were ask - ing for her hand. They'd of - fer her the moon and they'd of - fer her the sea. I off - ered her a sand - wich and she said she'd mar - ry me. (Chorus)
4. A sand - wich may by egg or cheese or ev - en peanut butter But they all taste so good to me, it real - ly doesn't matter. Jam or ham or cuc - um - ber, an - y kind will do. I like sand - wich - es, how a - bout you? (Chorus-twice)

78
She'll Be Comin' Round The Mountain

Traditional/Arranged by Mike Jackson

6. Oh we'll all have chicken and dumplings when she comes (Yum yum!)
(etc.)
(Chorus)

7. Oh we'll kill the old red rooster when she comes (Chop chop!)
(etc.)
(Chorus)

79
Silent Night

Traditional/Arranged by Mike Jackson

D A
1. Si - lent night, ho - ly night, All is calm,
2. Si - lent night, ho - ly night, Shep - herds quake
3. Si - lent night, ho - ly night, Son of God,
D D7 G D
all is bright. Round yon Vir - gin Moth - er and Child,
at the sight. Glor - ies stream from heaven a - far,
love's pure light. Rad - iant beams from Thy ho - ly face,
G D A
Ho - ly In - fant so tend - er and mild, Sleep in heaven - ly
Heav'n - ly hosts sing All - e - lu - ia; Christ the Sav - iour is
With the dawn of re - deem - ing, grace, Je - sus, Lord, at Thy
D Bm D A7 D
pea - ce; sleep in heaven - ly peace.
bor - n; Christ the Sav - iour is born.
bir - th; Jes - us, Lord, at Thy birth.

80
Slowly Going Crazy

Traditional/Arranged by Mike Jackson

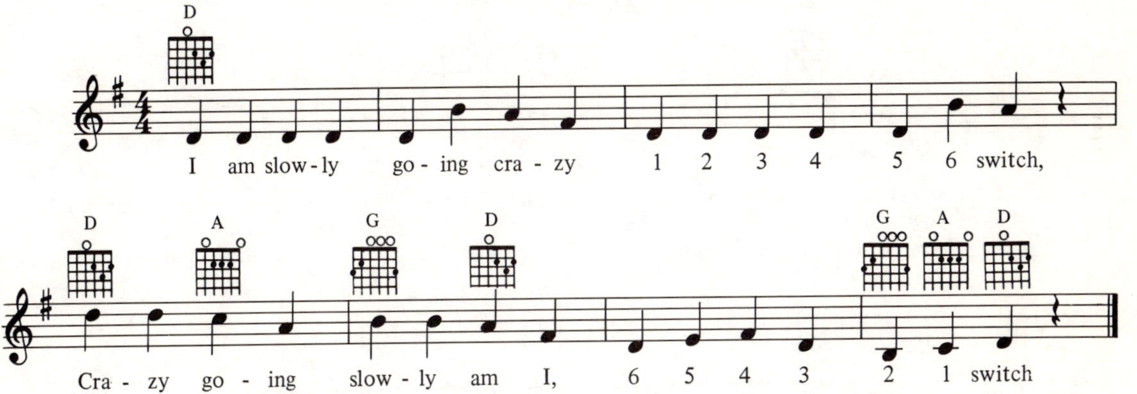
D
I am slow-ly go-ing cra-zy 1 2 3 4 5 6 switch,
D A G D G A D
Cra-zy go-ing slow-ly am I, 6 5 4 3 2 1 switch

(Sharon, Lois and Bram, three Canadian Children's Entertainers, have a delightful version of this song. One starts really slowly, the second sings twice as fast and the third twice as fast again. Crazy? Try it!)

81
Someone's In The Kitchen With Dinah

Traditional/Arranged by Mike Jackson

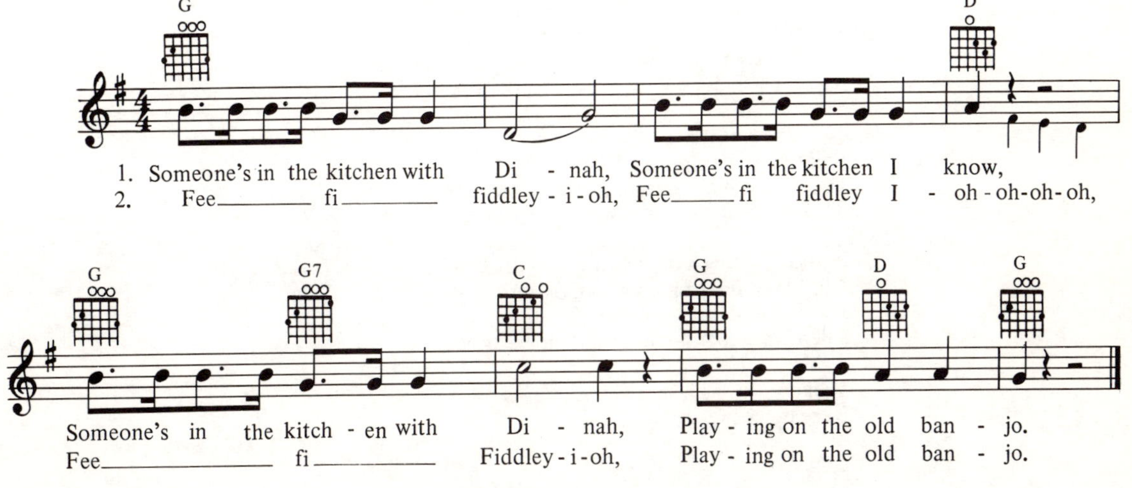
G D
1. Someone's in the kitchen with Di-nah, Someone's in the kitchen I know,
2. Fee fi fiddley-i-oh, Fee fi fiddley I-oh-oh-oh-oh,
G G7 C G D G
Someone's in the kitch-en with Di-nah, Play-ing on the old ban-jo.
Fee fi Fiddley-i-oh, Play-ing on the old ban-jo.

82
Spider On The Floor

Words & Music by Bill Russell

D
A7
1. There's a spi - der on the floor, on the floor. There's a spi-der on the floor, on the
2. Now the spi -der's on my leg, on my leg. Oh the spi-der's on my leg, on my
3. Now the spi -der's on my stomach, on my stomach. Oh the spi-der's on my stomach, on my
D
G
D
floor. Who could ask for an - y more than a spi - der on the floor, There's a
leg. Oh he's real - ly big! This old spi - der on my leg. There's a
stomach. Oh, he's just a dumb old lummock, this old spi - der on my stomach. There's a
A7
1.-6.
D
A7
7.
D
spi - der on the floor, on the floor. On the floor.
spi - der on my leg, on my leg.
spi - der on my stomach, on my stomach.

Modulate up a semitone with each verse for six verses.
Spoken phrase after verse 6, Verse 7 in original key.

4. Now the spider's on my neck, on my neck,
Oh, the spider's on my neck, on my neck.
Oh, I'm gonna be a wreck, I've got a spider on my neck.
There's a spider on my neck, on my neck.

5. Now the spider's on my face, on my face,
Oh, the spider's on my face, on my face.
Oh, what a big disgrace, I've got a spider on my face.
There's a spider on my face, on my face.

6. Now the spider's on my head, on my head,
Oh, the spider's on my head, on my head.
Oh, I wish that I were dead, I've got a spider on my head.
There's a spider on my head, on my head.

Spoken: But he jumps off. . . . . . .

7. Repeat 1st. Verse.

83
The Teddy Bears' Picnic

Words & Music by Jimmy Bratten & John W. Bratten

A
D7 Gm D7 Gm D7 Gm D7 Gm F7
If you go down in the woods to-day you're sure of a big sur - prise If
Bb F7 Bb F7 Bb F7 Bb
you go down in the woods to-day you'd bet-ter go in dis - guise for
F Fdim F7 Bb Eb Bb
Ev - 'ry bear that ev - er there was will gath - er there for cer-tain be-cause to -
Eb Bb Eb Bb F7 Bb
(1st time D7
2nd time Bb7)
day's the day the ted - dy bears have their pic - nic.
B
Eb Ebdim Eb
Pic - nic time for ted - dy bears the lit - tle ted - dy bears are
Bb7
hav-ing a love - ly time to - day.
Watch them, catch them
Bb Eb Bb7
un - a - wares and see them pic - nic on their hol - i - day!

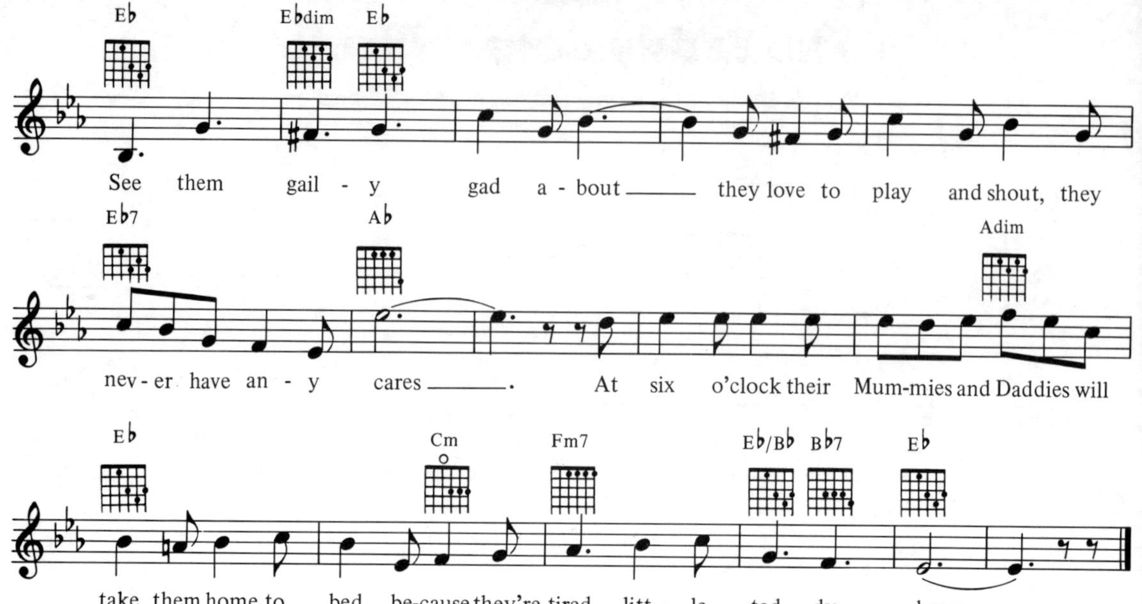
Eb
Ebdim
Eb
See them gail - y gad a - bout they love to play and shout, they
Eb7
Ab
Adim
nev - er have an - y cares. At six o'clock their Mum-mies and Daddies will
Eb
Cm
Fm7
Eb/Bb
Bb7
Eb
take them home to bed be-cause they're tired litt - le ted - dy bears.

A If you go down in the woods today you're sure of a big surprise
If you go down in the woods today you'd better go in disguise
For every bear that ever there was
Will gather there for certain because
Today's the day the Teddy Bears have their picnic.

A Every Teddy Bear who's been good is sure of a treat today
There's lots of marvellous things to eat and wonderful games to play
Beneath the trees where nobody sees
They hide and seek as long as they please
'Cos that's the way the Teddy Bears have their picnic.

A If you go down in the woods today you'd better not go alone
It's lovely down in the woods today but safer to stay at home
For every bear that ever there was will gather there for certain because
Today's the day the Teddy Bears have their picnic.

B Picnic time for Teddy Bears
The little Teddy Bears are having a lovely time today.
Watch them, catch them unawares
And see them picnic on their holiday!
See them gaily gad about
They love to play and shout, they never have any cares -
At six o'clock their Mummies and Daddies will take them home to bed
Because they're tired little Teddy Bears.

A If you go down in the woods today you'd better not go alone
It's lovely down in the woods today but safer to stay at home
For every bear that ever their was will gather there for certain because
Today's the day the Teddy Bears have their picnic.

84
Ten In The Bed

Traditional/Arranged by Mike Jackson

D G D G D
1. There were ten in the bed and the lit - tle one said, "Roll ov - er, roll
2. There were nine in the bed and the lit - tle one said, "Roll ov - er, roll
3. There were eight in the bed and the lit - tle one said, "Roll ov - er, roll
4. There were seven in the bed and the lit - tle one said, "Roll ov - er, roll
and so on down to
10. There was one in the bed and the lit - tle one said, "Roll ov - er, roll
11. There were none in the bed...... (Silence)
G D7 G C G D7 G
ov - er, so they all rolled ov - er, and one fell out

85
There's A Hole In The Bucket

Traditional/Arranged by Mike Jackson

G
C
Am
D7
HENRY: There's a hole in the buck - et, dear Li - za, dear Li - za, there's a hole in the buck - et, dear Li - za, a hole.
LIZA : Well, fix it, dear Hen - ry, dear Hen - ry, dear Hen- ry, then fix it dear Hen - ry, dear Hen - ry, fix it.
HENRY: With what shall I fix it, dear Li - za, dear Li - za, with what shall I fix it, dear Li - za, with what.
LIZA : With straw, dear Hen - ry, dear Hen - ry, dear Hen- ry, with with straw dear Hen - ry, dear Hen - ry, with straw..

HENRY: But the straw is too long, dear Liza, dear Liza,
But the straw is too long, dear Liza, too long.

LIZA: Well, cut it, dear Henry, dear Henry, dear Henry,
Well, cut it, dear Henry, dear Henry, cut it.

HENRY: With what shall I cut it.........

LIZA: With an axe.........

HENRY: But the axe is too blunt.........

LIZA: Well sharpen it.........

HENRY: With what shall I sharpen it.........

LIZA: With a stone.........

HENRY: But the stone is too dry.........

LIZA: Well wet it.........

HENRY: With what shall I wet it.........

LIZA: Try water.........

HENRY: In what shall I fetch it.........

LIZA: In a bucket.........

HENRY: But there's a hole in the bucket..........

86
This Old Man

Traditional/Arranged by Mike Jackson

G C D
This old man, he played one, he played knick knack on my drum, with a
This old man, he played two, he played knick knack on my shoe, with a
This old man, he played three, he played knick knack on my knee, with a
This old man, he played four, he played knick knack on my door, with a
G C G D D7 G
knick knack pad - dy whack, give a dog a bone, this old man came rol - ling home.

This old man, he played five,
He played knick knack on my hive,
With a knick knack paddy whack, give a dog a bone,
This old man came rolling home.

This old man, he played six,
He played knick knack on my sticks,
With a knick knack. . .

This old man, he played seven,
He played knick knack up in heaven,
With a knick knack. . .

This old man, he played eight,
He played knick knack on my gate,
With a knick knack. . .

This old man, he played nine,
He played knick knack on my spine,
With a knick knack. . .

This old man, he played ten,
He played knick knack home again,
With a knick knack. . .

87
A Thousand Hairy Savages

Words by Spike Milligan
Music by Ken Lees

Dm
A7
Dm
1
A thou - sand hair - y sav - a - ges, sit - ting down to lunch.
2
Gob - ble, gob - ble, gulp, gulp, munch, munch, munch.

88
Tiddy Lend Me Your Pigeon

Melody: Traditional/Arranged by Mike Jackson
Verses 1, 2 & 3: Traditional
Verses 4, 5 & 6: Added by Mike & Michelle Jackson

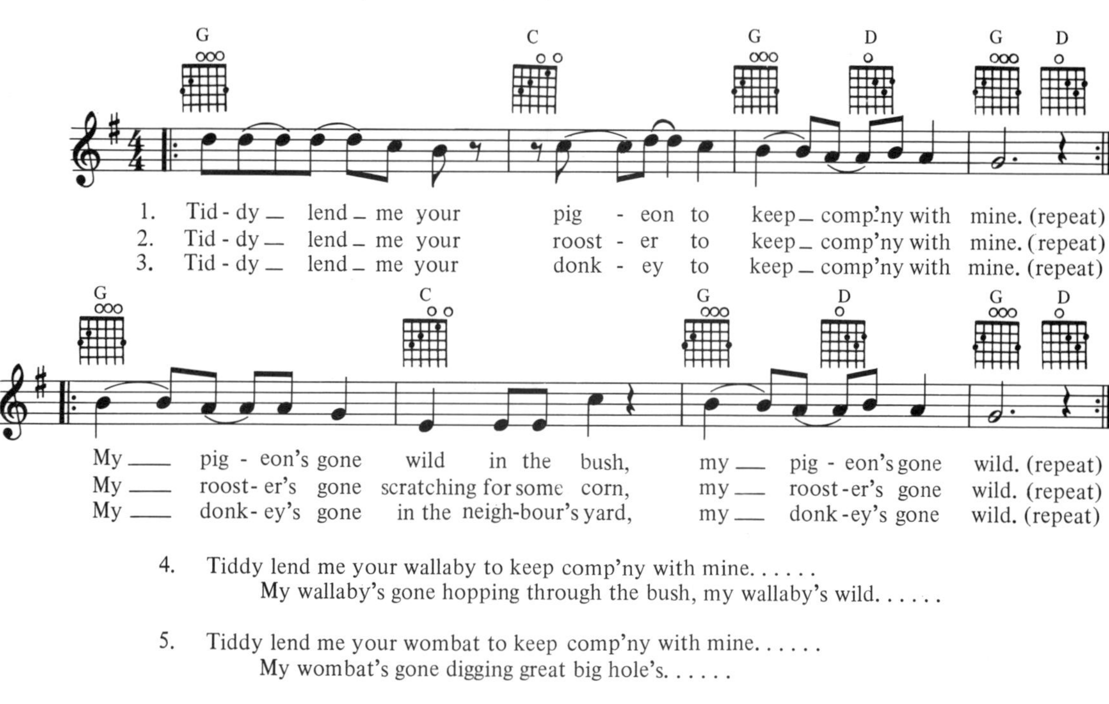

G
C
G
D
G
D
1. Tid - dy lend me your pig - eon to keep comp'ny with mine. (repeat)
2. Tid - dy lend me your roost - er to keep comp'ny with mine. (repeat)
3. Tid - dy lend me your donk - ey to keep comp'ny with mine. (repeat)
My pig - eon's gone wild in the bush, my pig - eon's gone wild. (repeat)
My roost - er's gone scratching for some corn, my roost - er's gone wild. (repeat)
My donk - ey's gone in the neigh - bour's yard, my donk - ey's gone wild. (repeat)

4. Tiddy lend me your wallaby to keep comp'ny with mine. . . . . .
   My wallaby's gone hopping through the bush, my wallaby's wild. . . . . .

5. Tiddy lend me your wombat to keep comp'ny with mine. . . . . .
   My wombat's gone digging great big hole's. . . . . .

6. Tiddy lend me your possum to keep com'ny with mine. . . . . .
   My possum's gone climbing in the trees. . . . .

7. So Tiddy lend me your pigeon to keep comp'ny with mine. . . . . .
   My pigeon's gone wild in the bush. . . . . . .

89
Tiddalik

Words & Music by Andrew Richardson

G
D7
1. Tid - da - lik, the big green frog, Spends all day
2. Tid - da - lik, one day was dry, He hadn't had a drink
3. Soon the land was very dry, The birds and the animals
4. The wom - bat said, 'Let's make him laugh, He'll giggle out the water, and
sit - ting on a log. In the morn - ings and the eve - nings —
for a long long time. He drank up the riv - ers and he drank up the
thought they might die. They walked across the desert and the dry creek —
we'll all take a bath, 'So they danced and they tick - led and they pranced all —
too, He likes to sing a lit - tle song to you, He goes croak,
streams, And the lakes and the Water - holes it seems. He went gulp,
beds, And gathered round Tidd - a - lik and all at once said, 'We want a drink,
a-round, But all old Tidd - a - lik could do was frown, He went frown,
croak, croak, croak, croak, croak, croak, croak, croak, croak,
gulp, gulp, gulp, gulp, gulp, gulp, gulp, gulp, gulp,
drink, drink, drink, drink, drink, drink, drink, drink, drink,
frown, frown, frown, frown, frown, frown, frown, frown, frown.

5. The kookaburra laughed and the kangaroo hopped,
And the little koala did a bob-ship-bop,
The emu said,
'The splits are fun,'
But landed up sitting on his round tum tum,
He said ouch, ouch, ouch, ouch, ouch,
ouch, ouch, ouch, ouch, ouch.

6. Tiddalik did a big belly laugh,
And the animals said, 'Here comes our bath!'
He gushed and he poured
and they drank and drank,
But poor old Tiddalik shrank and shrank,
They went splish, splash, taking a bath,
splish, splash, splish, splash, splish, splash.

90
Threw It Out The Window

Traditional/Arranged by Mike Jackson

G
1. Lit - tle Jack Hor - ner sat in a cor - ner eat - ing his Christ - mas
2. Old Jim Jones is a jol - ly old soul and a jol - ly old soul is

D
pie. He stuck in his thumb and pulled out a plum and
he. So I'll help you if you'll help me to

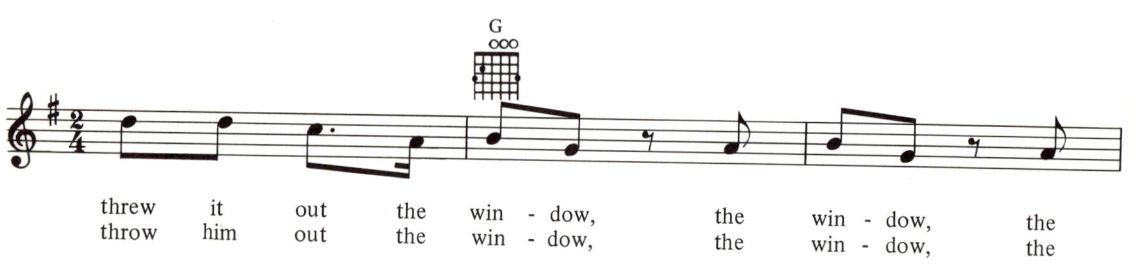
G
threw it out the win - dow, the win - dow, the
throw him out the win - dow, the win - dow, the

D
sec - ond sto - rey win - dow, with a heave and a ho and a
sec - ond sto - rey win - dow, with a heave and a ho and a

G
heave heave ho he threw it out the win - dow.
heave heave ho we'll throw him out the win - dow.

91
Turkey In The Straw

Words: Traditional/Adapted by Mike Jackson
Music: Traditional/Arranged by Mike Jackson

D7
G
1. Well I had a lit - tle chick - en and it wouldn't lay an egg So I
2. Well I had an - oth - er chick - en and she wouldn't lay an egg So I
3. Well I went to Ood - na - dat - ta and I walked a-long the street And I
4. Well she looked at the co - in and she looked at me

D
G
poured hot wat - er all down the chick-en's leg, Well the little chick-en cried and the
ran a bus up and down the chick-en's leg, Well the little chick-en cried and the
went into the bak-er's shop to buy my - self a treat. I lift - ed a dough - nut
Said, "This mon-ey's no good to me. There's hole in the mid-dle and it

G
D
G
lit - tle chick-en begged And the darned old chick-en laid a hard - boiled egg!
lit - tle chick-en begged And the darned old chick-en laid a bust - ed egg!
out of the grease And I handed the lady there a five cent piece.
goes right through." Says I, "There's a hole in the dough - nut too.

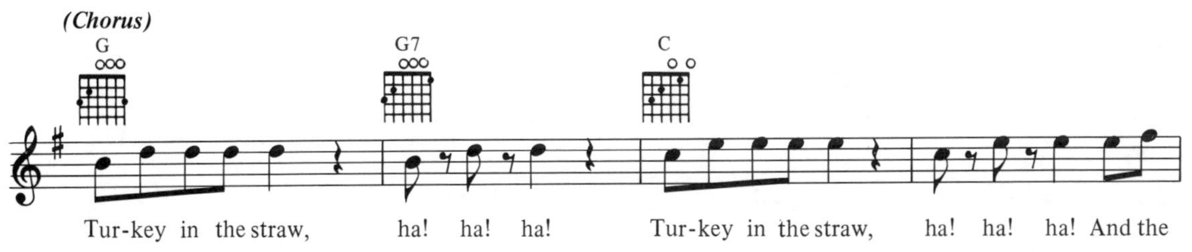

(Chorus)
G
G7
C
Tur-key in the straw, ha! ha! ha! Tur-key in the straw, ha! ha! ha! And the

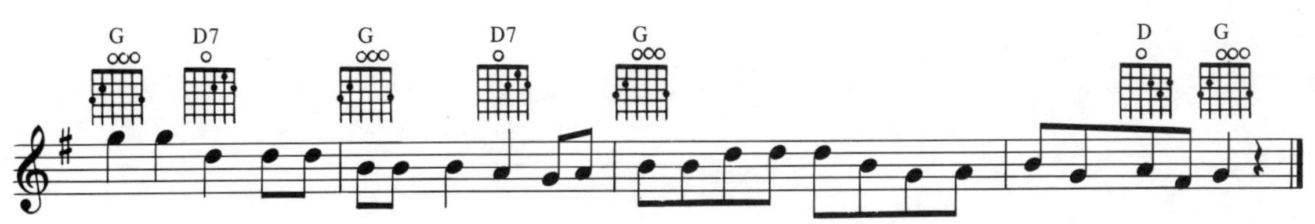

G
D7
G
D7
G
D
G
old folks dance with the mo-ther-in - law and they do a lit- tle dance they call the Turkey in the Straw.

92
Twinkle Twinkle Little Star

Traditional/Arranged by Mike & Michelle Jackson

D G D A7 D Bm
1. Twin - kle, twin - kle, li - ttle star, how I won - der
2. Twin - kle, twin - kle, li - ttle star, Dad - dy bought a
3. Twin - kle, twin - kle, li - ttle moon, how I hope to
4. Twin - kle, twin - kle, li - ttle moon, how I won - der
Em A7 D Em D A7
what you are. Up a - bove the world so high,
mot - or car. Press the but - ton, pull the choke,
see you soon. In our lit - tle ro - cket ship,
what you're doin'. Up a - bove the world so high,
D Em D A7 D D7
like a dia - mond in the sky. Twin - kle, twin - kle,
off we go in a cloud of smoke,(cough) Twin - kle, twin - kle,
won't we have a love - ly trip. Twin - kle, twin - kle,
like a pan - cake in the sky! Twin - kle, twin - kle,
G F#m Em D G6 A7 D
lit - tle star, How I won - der what you are.
lit - tle star, Dad - dy bought a mot - or car.
lit - tle moon, Hope that you can come back soon.
lit - tle moon, How I won - der what you're doin'.

93
Waltzing Matilda

Words: A.B. Paterson   Music: Traditional/Setting Arranged by M. Cowan

D A Bm G D
1. Once a jol - ly swag - man, cam - ped by a bill - a - bong, Un - der the
2. Down came a jum - buck to drink at that bill - a - bong, Up jumped the
3. Up rode the squat - ter mounted on his thor-ough-bred Down came the
4. Up jumped the swagman and sprang into the bill - a - bong, "You'll nev - er
Bm Em A7 D A7
shade of a cool - i - bah tree, And he sang as he watched and
swag-man and grab - bed him with glee, And he sang as he shoved that
troop-ers one, two, three, 'Whose is that jum - buck
catch me a - live, said he. And his ghost may be heard as you
Bm G D Bm G A7 D
wait - ed till his bill - y boiled
jum-buck in his tuck - er bag
you've got in your tuck - er bag
pass by that bill - a-bong,
You'll come a waltz - ing Ma - til - da with me.
Chorus
D D7 G Em F♯m Bm
Waltz - ing Ma - til - da, Waltz - ing Ma - til - da You'll come a Waltz - ing Ma -
G A7 D A7 Bm
til - da with me,
1. And he sang as he watched and wait - ed till his
2. And he sang as he shoved that jum - buck in his
3. 'Whose is that jum - buck you've got in your
4. And his ghost may be heard as you pass by that
G D Bm G A7 D
bill - y boiled,
tuck - er bag,
tuck - er bag,
bill - a - bong,
You'll come a Waltz - ing Ma - til - da with me.

94
Watermelon Song

Traditional/Arranged by Mike Jackson

D
You can plant a wat - er-mel - on up a - bove my grave and let the
A
D
juice (SLURP) seep through you can plant a wat - er-mel - on up a-
D
A
E7
A7
bove my grave thats all I ask of you well
D
D7
G
choco-late chip cook-ies taste migh - ty fine but theres noth - ing quite as good as a
Gm
D
wat - er mel - on vine, you can plant a wat - er mel - on up a -
A
D
bove my grave and let the juice (SLURP) seep through.

[The "(SLURP!)" should be the biggest juiciest "slurping" sound you can make.]

95

We Wish You A Merry Christmas

Traditional/Arranged by Mike Jackson

G C A7 D7

1. We wish you a Mer-ry Christ - mas, we wish you a Mer-ry Christ - mas, We
2. We all like fig - gy pud - ding, we all like fig -gy pud -ding, We
3. We won't go un- til we've got some, we won't go un - til we've got some,We
4. We wish you a Mer- ry Christ - mas, we wish you a Mer-ry Christ - mas, We

B7 Em C D G D

wish you a Mer-ry Christ - mas and a Hap - py New Year.
all like fig -gy pud - ding, please bring some out here.
won't go un - til we've got some, please bring some out here.
wish you a Mer -ry Christ-mas and a Hap - py New Year.

Good tid-ings we bring to

A7 D G C D G

you and your kin. We wish you a Mer-ry Christ - mas and a Hap - py New Year.

96

Where Oh Where Has My Little Dog Gone

Traditional/Arranged by Mike Jackson

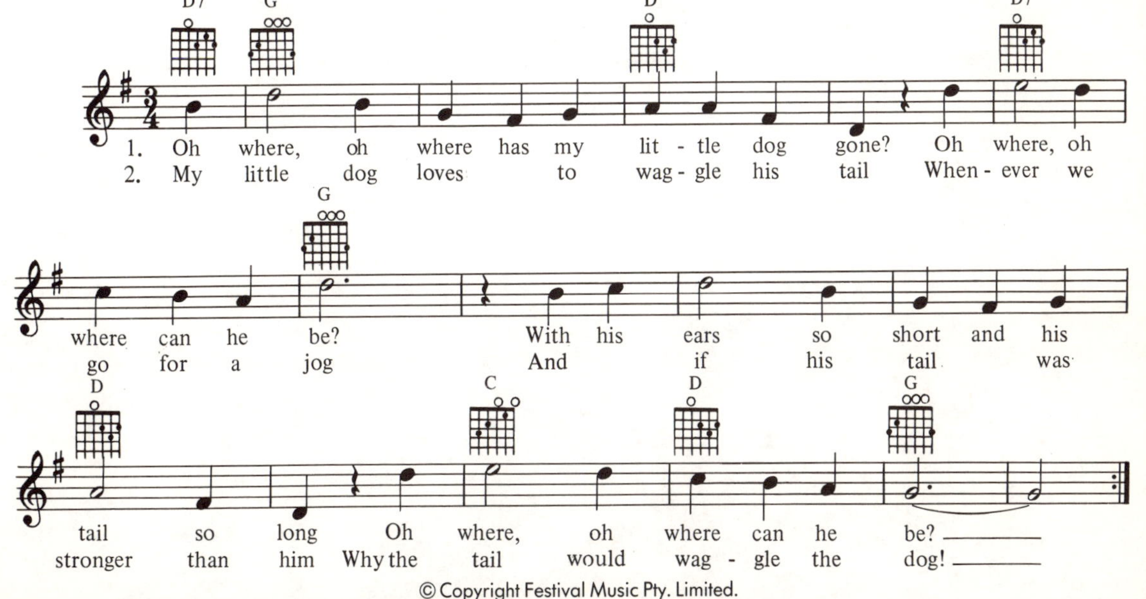
D7 G D D7
1. Oh where, oh where has my lit - tle dog gone? Oh where, oh
2. My little dog loves to wag - gle his tail When - ever we
G
where can he be? With his ears so short and his
go for a jog And if his tail was
D C D G
tail so long Oh where, oh where can he be?
stronger than him Why the tail would wag - gle the dog!

97
While Shepherds Watched Their Flocks By Night

Nahum Tate/Arranged by Mike Jackson

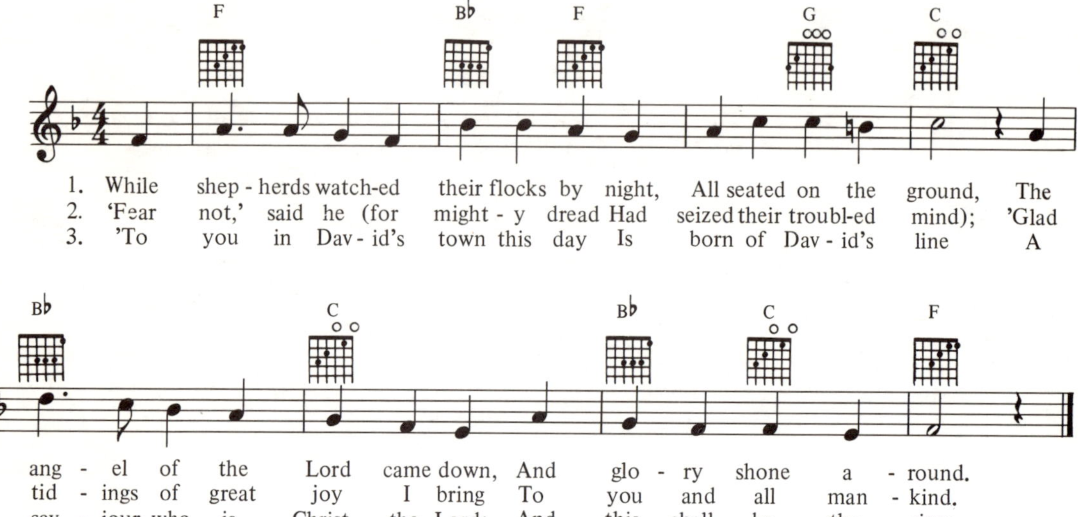

F
B♭
F
G
C
1. While shep - herds watch-ed their flocks by night, All seated on the ground, The
2. 'Fear not,' said he (for might - y dread Had seized their troubl-ed mind); 'Glad
3. 'To you in Dav - id's town this day Is born of Dav - id's line A
B♭
C
B♭
C
F
ang - el of the Lord came down, And glo - ry shone a - round.
tid - ings of great joy I bring To you and all man - kind.
sav - iour, who is Christ the Lord; And this shall be the sign:

4. 'The heavenly babe you there shall find
   To human view displayed,
   All meanly wrapped in swathing bands,
   And in a manger laid.'

5. Thus spake the seraph: and forthwith
   Appeared a shining throng
   Of angels praising God, who thus
   Addressed their joyful song:

6. 'All glory be to God on high,
   And to the earth be peace;
   Goodwill henceforth from heaven to men.
   Begin and never cease.

98
Why Does It Have To Be Me?

Words & Music by Leon Rosselson

C G7 C F
Why does it have to be me? Why can't they just let me be?
F Repeat after last Chorus G7 C G7 C Verse
Why do I have to do things I don't want to do? Why does it have to be me? 1. Each
C G7 C F
morn - ing I lie in my bed, Slip - per - y dreams in my head. I
2. Why do I have to eat greens? Cab - bage and spin - ach and beans? I
3. Why can't I play my own games? Some-bod - y al - ways com - plains, When
F C G7 C
live in a fine fai - ry cas - tle of stone all on my own, no - one to moan. Then a
don't mind potatoes, I'll even have meat, Tho' I'd much rather eat Icecreams and sweets, They say
ev - er I'm play-ing at mon-sters or bears, jump - ing off chairs, fall - ing down stairs,
F C F
voice shouts, 'Get up!' and it is - n't dream. 'Hur-ry up you're late for school and wash your face and brush your
greens are good for me, May - be they're right some - times I think that they
It's 'don't be so noisy' or 'go out and play' Or 'look at a book if you're
C F
teeth and are your fin - gers clean? And they go on and on till I'm
do it for spite, And I've ne - ver seen them eat - ing
go - ing to stay.' The prob - lem is they al - ways
C G7 C
rea - dy to scream. Why does it have to be me? (Chorus)
what they don't like, Why does it have to be me? (Chorus)
get in my way, So why does it have to be me? (Chorus)

99
The Wrong End

Traditional/Arranged by Mike Jackson

G
C
G
Rab - bits have bright shin - ey nos - es, I'm
G
D
G
tell - ing you this as a friend, the rea - son their
C
G
A7
D7
no - ses are shi - ney the pow - der puff's on the wrong
G
G7
C
A7
end Wrong end, wrong end, the
D
G
pow - der puff's on the wrong end, wrong end, wrong end,
C
A7
D
G
wrong end, the pow - der puff's on the wrong end.

100
Yellow Submarine

Words & Music by John Lennon & Paul McCartney

F C7 Bb F Dm Gm Bb C7
In the town where I was born Lived a man who sailed to sea. And he
C7 Bb F Dm Gm Bb C7 F
told us of his life in the land of sub-mar-ines. So we
C7 Bb F Dm Gm Bb C7 F
sailed on to the sun. Till we found the sea of green. And we
C7 Bb F Dm Gm Bb C7
lived be-neath the waves in our Yel low sub-mar-ine
F Chorus C7 F
We all live in a Yel-low sub-mar-ine. Yel-low sub-mar-ine. Yel-low sub-mar-ine.
F C7 F Fine
We all live in a Yel-low sub-mar-ine. Yel-low sub-mar-ine. Yel-low sub-mar-ine.
F C7 Bb F Dm Gm Bb C7 F
2. And our friends are all a-board. Ma-ny more of them live next door. And the
3. As we live a life of ease. Eve-ry one of us has all we need. Sky of
C7 Bb F Dm Gm Bb C7 D.S. al Fine
band be-gins to play (imitation of band playing)
blue and sea of green in our Yel-low sub-mar-ine.

101

You'll Never Get To Heaven

Traditional/Arranged by Mike Jackson
1. Oh you'll never get to heaven (Oh you'll never get to heaven) On a rol-ler skate (On a rol-ler
2. Oh you'll never get to heaven (Oh you'll never get to heaven) In a roc-ket ship (On a roc-ket
3. Oh you'll never get to heaven (Oh you'll never get to heaven) On an old tram car (On an old tram
4. Oh you'll never get to heaven (Oh you'll never get to heaven) In a Lim-ous - ine (In a lim-ous-
5. Oh you'll never get to heaven (Oh you'll never get to heaven) With Sup-er -man (With Sup-er -
unison
skate) 'Cos a rol-ler skate ('Cos a rol-ler skate) Would be too late (Would be too late) Oh you'll never get to
ship) 'Cos a roc-ket ship ('Cos a rocket ship) Won't make the trip! (Won't make the trip) Oh you'll never get to
car) 'Cos an old tram car ('Cos an old tram car) Won't get that far! (Won't get that far) Oh you'll never get to
ine) 'Cos the Lord don't sell ('Cos the Lord don't sell) No gas-o- line! (No gas - o - line) Oh you'll never get to
man) 'Cos the Lord he is ('Cos the Lord he is) A Bat-man fan! (A Bat-man man) Oh you'll never get to
heav-en on a rol - ler skate 'cos a rol - ler skate would be too late.
heav-en in a roc - ket ship 'cos a roc - ket ship won't make the trip.
heav-en on an old tram car 'cos an old tram car won't get that far.
heav-en in a Lim - ous - ine 'cos the Lord don't sell no gas - o - line.
heav-en with Sup - er - man 'cos the Lord he is a Bat -man man.
I ain't a gon-na
Chorus
grieve my Lord no more. I ain't a gon - na grieve my
lord. I ain't a gon- na grieve my Lord. I ain't a gon-na grieve my Lord no
more no more I ain't a gonna grieve my Lord I ain't a gon- na grieve my
Lord I ain't a gonna grieve my lord no more!